D1488950

# THE PITTSBURGH STEELERS PLAYBOOK

Inside the Huddle for the
Greatest Plays in Steelers History

Steve Hickoff

TRIUMPH
B O O K S

*This book is dedicated to my father, who, like other fans at the time, first watched the Pittsburgh Steelers at Forbes Field in the franchise's early days and truly earned the Super Bowl glory years that followed.*

---

Copyright © 2015 by Steve Hickoff

No part of this publication may be reproduced, stored in a retrieval system, or transmitted in any form by any means, electronic, mechanical, photocopying, or otherwise, without the prior written permission of the publisher, Triumph Books LLC, 814 North Franklin Street, Chicago, Illinois 60610.

Material previously published in the book *The 50 Greatest Plays in Pittsburgh Steelers Football History* © 2008 by Steve Hickoff (Chicago: Triumph Books)

This book is available in quantity at special discounts for your group or organization. For further information, contact:

**Triumph Books LLC**
814 North Franklin Street
Chicago, Illinois 60610
(312) 337-0747
www.triumphbooks.com

Printed in U.S.A.
ISBN: 978-1-62937-124-5
Design by Andy Hansen

# CONTENTS

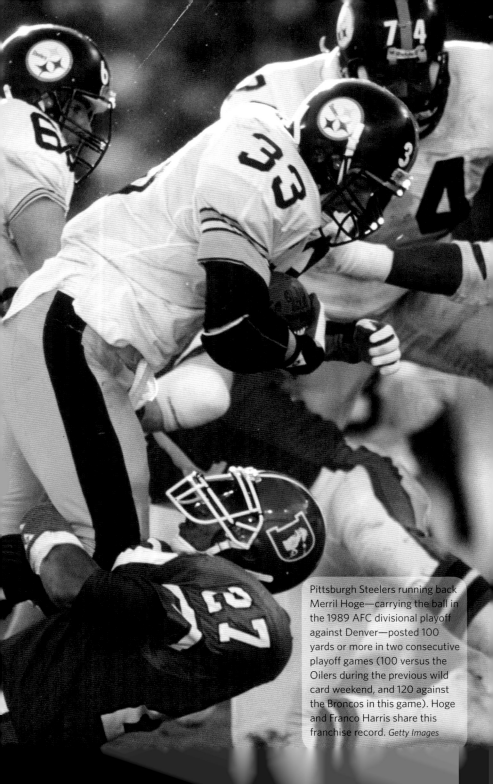

Pittsburgh Steelers running back Merril Hoge—carrying the ball in the 1989 AFC divisional playoff against Denver—posted 100 yards or more in two consecutive playoff games (100 versus the Oilers during the previous wild card weekend, and 120 against the Broncos in this game). Hoge and Franco Harris share this franchise record. *Getty Images*

# ACKNOWLEDGMENTS

**D**uring the writing of this manuscript, I lived with the written facts, play photos, and game films, cross-referencing dated and recent material in an effort to get it right, paying obsessive attention to details as all serious NFL fans do—the only difference here is that you can hold the result in your hands.

But no writer works alone. Thanks are due...

First of all to editor, writer, friend, and football fan Don Gulbrandsen who encouraged this project from start to finish, as well as Tom Bast, Mitch Rogatz, and everyone else at Triumph Books. I'm honored to have been involved in this enterprise.

Thanks especially to my wife, Elizabeth, and our daughter, Cora.

My family members, immediate and extended—many are Steelers fans, of course—deserve notice as well.

As a longtime fan, my personal appreciation also goes out to the Pittsburgh Steelers franchise—an extension of the late Art Rooney's original vision—and the former and current players. Speaking for other members of Steelers Nation, we take pride in the Black and Gold football legacy.

Crafting this NFL football history into final book form required sustained effort—a process I enjoyed both as a professional writer and devoted follower of the team. In the end, I hope *The Pittsburgh Steelers Playbook* revives some personal memories for you and adds some new ones.

It all began in 1933 when the cigar-chomping Arthur J. Rooney, also known as "The Chief"—a tavern owner's son from Pittsburgh's North Side, amateur athlete, and, most of all, sports promoter—committed $2,500 to the upstart National Football League. Rooney's Pittsburgh Pirates later became the Steelers. *Getty Images*

# INTRODUCTION

**H**ard-core fans of the Black and Gold will understand why the top two greatest Pittsburgh Steelers plays of all time involve a running back catching a pass that wasn't intended for him and a quarterback making a tackle to save a season.

It all began in 1933 when Arthur J. Rooney, also known as "the Chief"—a tavern owner's son from Pittsburgh's North Side, amateur athlete, and, most of all, a sports promoter—committed $2,500 to the upstart National Football League. Rooney's Depression-era investment marks the beginning of this historical franchise, born from steel mills, coal mines, and hard living.

Pittsburgh's first postseason appearance came in the 1947 NFL Eastern division championship against the Philadelphia Eagles. Since then the Steelers franchise has won five Super Bowls, starting with the Steel Curtain teams of the 1970s.

Unexpected drama unites the NFL fans of Steelers Nation. I've tried to capture those memories in this book, whether it's material on offensive Super Bowl standouts Lynn Swann and John Stallworth or defensive Hall of Fame players Jack Ham, Mel Blount, and Jack Lambert. I've included plays such as the Immaculate Reception, Willie Parker's 75-yard Super Bowl XL run from scrimmage, and a kickoff fumble recovery on the rain-soaked Three Rivers Stadium turf in the 1978 AFC championship when the Pittsburgh Steelers scored 17 points in under a minute.

There's Pittsburgh kicker Gary Anderson drilling a 50-yard field goal in overtime. Quarterback Mark Malone's record-setting *catch* of 90 yards from Terry Bradshaw. John Henry Johnson running for a 45-yard touchdown to lead the Steelers to a 23–7 upset of their rivals, the Cleveland Browns. Linebacker Andy Russell's fumble recovery and 93-yard jog for a touchdown to clinch the 1975 AFC divisional playoff win. Kordell Stewart connecting on a shovel pass to Jerome Bettis, who ran 17 untouched yards for the touchdown and overtime victory. Even Ernie Stautner's hard-nosed tackle on Giants third-string quarterback and future Dallas Cowboys coach Tom Landry during a 63–7 Steelers win. No typo there—that was quite the rout.

These 50 plays include a range of highs and lows, the thrilling wins and even some losses, the interceptions, passes, and catches, the fumbles, field goals, touchdowns, and even one Super Bowl safety—the first in the big game's history.

There's plenty to savor here—objective facts and subjective observations, memorable quotes, statistics, play diagrams, and even pop-culture connections. I hope some obscure historical details are new to you and add to your appreciation of the Pittsburgh Steelers.

I chose plays based on a number of factors, attempting to rank important wins over the years. Rivalries were considered. In certain cases, a play during the regular season or playoffs that later made a Super Bowl victory possible often ranked higher in my mind than a memorable moment during a championship game. I mixed old plays with new, success with a dash of heartbreak. Records were noted. Several plays that involve opposing quarterbacks falling short of their intentions are included. At times, a seemingly less dramatic play, though still great in importance, is highlighted at the start or end of a series of others in certain games—in several cases big comebacks from scoring deficits.

Exciting touchdown runs and tackles naturally made the cut, most often after I viewed those filmed plays over and over again, a time-travel process I thoroughly enjoyed. You'll note my penchant for representing good, solid defense here, and unexpected game events, particularly if the Steelers benefited. After all, this sort of stuff makes us stand up and yell at the television screen. As a result, Pittsburgh kickers get some serious game-winning attention as well.

Yes, I also had some plays that didn't make the top 50 cut, and I'm sure some of my selections and rankings will be contested by Steelers diehards out there—a welcome condition, as such conversations fuel the tradition.

Born in Pennsylvania in 1958 and raised north of Pittsburgh, I've experienced many solid Steelers seasons. As a lifelong fan, I'm glad to have had the opportunity to write this kind of book. Like some of you, I enjoyed the first two Super Bowl wins—as a Keystone State high-school student in my case. I also watched the second two victories during my Pennsylvania college days. Like you, I suffered through the tough years too, enjoying the highlights along the way.

February 11, 2001, the day they blew up Three Rivers Stadium to pave the way for Heinz Field, was bittersweet for some of us, as many a memorable Steelers game took place in that old stadium between 1970 and 2000. But time added more memories. The fifth championship—finally one for the thumb, and the first Pittsburgh Super Bowl win of this century—punctuated the end of an amazing playoff run. Local Steelers fans and I gathered at a sports bar for that one.

Black and Gold backers got a ring for the other hand in Super Bowl XLIII, though our loyalty to the team remains no matter what. This is more than just being a football fan—it's a lifestyle founded on an appreciation of the team's history and deep cultural connections based on geography and birthright, homegrown or not. Pittsburgh Steelers fans live all over the world.

Selecting the memorable events that make up *The Pittsburgh Steelers Playbook* has been an enormous pleasure that afforded me an excuse to relive these moments again and again. I hope you enjoy reading the book as much as I enjoyed writing it.

# WHEN IT MATTERED MOST

# HARRISON INTERCEPTS AND RUNS INTO SUPER BOWL HISTORY

James Harrison records the longest return in Super Bowl history by a defender

**W**hen the subject of Super Bowl XLIII comes up amongst Steelers fans, they talk about two specific plays. This one, dubbed the "The Immaculate Interception"—a riff on Franco Harris's legendary and iconic Immaculate Reception in 1972—came on the last play of the first half.

It shifted momentum dramatically.

But first, a word or two on the Steelers' playoff run after their dominating 12–4 regular season in 2008, good enough to finish first in the AFC North.

In their January 11 division game against San Diego, the Steelers rolled over the Chargers 35–24 as snow flurries floated down at Heinz

Field. Next up, they'd face the rival Baltimore Ravens for the AFC championship.

Hard hitting? It's a given when these two meet. Defense wins championships, they say. Troy Polamalu's interception and dramatic run to the end zone clinched it. Final score: Steelers 23, Ravens 14.

Next, they'd fly south out of the cold Pennsylvania winter to Florida, where the Arizona Cardinals would be waiting to meet them.

In Super Bowl XLIII, Pittsburgh's offense dominated early, with Ben Roethlisberger leading the team to a 10–0 lead. Their time of possession ruled. But wait. The Cardinals didn't just roll over and quit. They'd come too far for that.

Steelers linebacker James Harrison returns an interception for a 100-yard touchdown during the second quarter of Super Bowl XLIII in 2009. Harrison's romp was the longest play in Super Bowl history by a defender. *AP Images*

In the second quarter, Arizona woke up: Kurt Warner hit Anquan Boldin for a reception and long downfield gain. The journeyman quarterback's short touchdown pass to Ben Patrick and an extra point by Neil Rackers pulled the Cardinals within three.

Then, suddenly it seemed, with just 18 seconds left in the first half, Warner—who'd been Super Bowl XXXIV MVP with "The Greatest Show on Turf" St. Louis Rams—seemed ready to put his team in the lead. Steelers fans felt the early excitement and momentum slipping away. It was time for the defense to step up as it had in the regular season and playoffs. It was time for a big stop.

One yard separated Arizona from the lead. First and goal.

One man would stop it.

Steelers showed blitz, but...

It could have been so different. Wary of the Steelers defense, Warner tried to push a quick red zone pass to Boldin. As if clairvoyant, James Harrison stepped in front of the effort, caught the ball, and lumbered hard down the near sideline. The longest interception return in Super Bowl history—exactly 100 yards—saw the Steelers linebacker eluding tackles (including an ineffective and stumbling attempt by Warner) and a big hit just before reaching the goal line.

Touchdown, right? It wasn't official yet.

Tense seconds passed for Steelers fans—and then the good news came. Touchdown, Steelers. Pittsburgh now had a 17–7 lead heading into the locker room. Instead of trailing Arizona, they enjoyed a 10-point lead. Wow.

You watched the televised replay unfold, at times in slow motion, as the Steelers defense turned toward the offensive, with players now blocking and Harrison moving the ball toward the opposite end zone. Relief and amazement followed. But it didn't come as a surprise to everyone. The Steelers had practiced such a play during drills.

James Harrison, the model of a linebacker at 6'0" and 242 pounds, found himself in an unusual position of the man with the ball. For Steelers fans, this was a little reminiscent of Andy Russell's recovery and long touchdown run after Jack Ham forced a Colts fumble to clinch the 1975 AFC divisional playoff win at Three Rivers Stadium.

Russell had returned the ball 93 yards on that occasion. In each instance, decades apart, both big men were clearly winded, with Harrison putting an oxygen mask to his face after running the length of the football field. Wouldn't you?

As mentioned, Harrison's interception and run for a touchdown is one of the great plays Steelers fans talk about when the subject of Super Bowl XLIII comes up. The one to win the game was just as thrilling.

# Game Details

## Pittsburgh 27 • Arizona 23

**Location:** Raymond James Stadium, Tampa, Florida

**Attendance:** 70,774

**Box Score:**

| | | | | | |
|---|---|---|---|---|---|
| **Steelers** | 3 | 14 | 3 | 7 | **27** |
| **Cardinals** | 0 | 7 | 0 | 16 | **23** |

*Scoring:*
PIT Reed 18-yard FG
PIT Russell 1-yard run (Reed PAT)
ARI Patrick 1-yard pass from Warner (Rackers PAT)
PIT Harrison 100-yard interception return (Reed PAT)
PIT Reed 21-yard FG
ARI Fitzgerald 1-yard pass from Warner (Rackers PAT)
ARI Safety (Hartwig penalized for holding in the end zone)
ARI Fitzgerald 64-yard pass from Warner (Rackers PAT)
PIT Holmes 6-yard pass from Roethlisberger (Reed PAT)

| Team | FD | RUSH | A-C-I | PASS |
|---|---|---|---|---|
| **Steelers** | 20 | 26/58 | 30-21-1 | 256 |
| **Cardinals** | 23 | 12/33 | 43-31-1 | 377 |

# ROETHLISBERGER TO HOLMES FOR THE WIN

After a dramatic drive, Big Ben and Santonio Holmes beat the Cardinals in Super Bowl XLIII

**T**he James Harrison interception and 100-yard return for a touchdown to end the first half of Super Bowl XLIII surely shifted momentum. Jeff Reed kicked the extra point and the Steelers entered the locker room feeling pretty good. But this game wasn't even close to over.

Leading 17–7, Pittsburgh added three more points on a 21-yard Reed field goal, the only scoring by either team during the third quarter. Maybe the Steelers were feeling a little too confident with their 20–7 lead. Maybe they were already visualizing raising the Lombardi Trophy. Because what came next from the Cardinals was anything but expected—though maybe it should have been.

The Cardinals, after all, were the highest scoring team in the postseason. The NFL's best defense had kept them in check for most of the game at least, but eventually Arizona broke through again. Kurt Warner and wide receiver Larry Fitzgerald—who played his college ball at

Steelers quarterback Ben Roethlisberger hugs wide receiver Santonio Holmes after their game-winning touchdown in the fourth quarter of Super Bowl XLIII. *AP Images*

Pitt—connected on a one-yard completion for an Arizona touchdown, followed by the extra point. Steelers 20, Cardinals 14.

And then the unthinkable: backed into their own end zone on the 1-yard line, with the Arizona defense now looking hungry as ever, Pittsburgh lineman Justin Hartwig was penalized for holding. The Cardinals got two points on the safety and would get the ball back, with the Steelers only leading by four.

Ben Roethlisberger completed 21 of 30 passes for 256 yards, with one interception and one touchdown—the game-winning pass to Santonio Holmes. *AP Images*

As if still stunned by the Pittsburgh offense's inability to contain the slipping Super Bowl momentum, the defense watched as Warner hit Fitzgerald over the middle and run 64 uncontested yards to the end zone. Rackers extra point: Cardinals 23, Steelers 20. Only 2:37 was left in the fourth quarter. Arizona fans in the stands seemed giddy with thoughts of their team winning at the wire. Was there enough time for Big Ben to pull out the win?

Maybe the Cardinals had scored too quickly. Maybe they'd left just a little bit too much time on the clock.

"Time to be great," Steelers wide receiver Santonio Holmes kept saying to his teammates. "Time to be great."

But to cover 78 yards with just over two minutes left? Yep, some greatness would be needed from Big Ben—and fast. Ever elusive, the linebacker-sized quarterback dodged the rush and hit Holmes for a completion. Then he hit him again for another big gain, down inside the 10-yard line. This almost looked like it was scripted.

With just 48 seconds left on the clock, Roethlisberger put a pass right on the mark to Holmes, who stretched high in the end zone—but it sailed through his hands. Oh, what could have been...

Down by three, now just 42 seconds left, second-and-goal at the 6-yard line, an undaunted Roethlisberger targeted Holmes in the same way this time—another perfect throw into the corner of the end zone. This time, both toes down, with three Cardinals defenders looking on: touchdown, Steelers.

But the Cardinals still had a chance. Warner completed two passes, but following Arizona's third timeout, he was sacked by LaMarr Woodley and fumbled the football.

Pittsburgh took possession, Roethlisberger took a knee, and that was it.

Santonio Holmes was named Super Bowl XLIII MVP, and the "Six-Burgh" Steelers now had a half-dozen NFL championships.

# STEELERS DEMOTE DENVER

The Pittsburgh defense finishes the job in the 2005 AFC Championship Game, claiming Jake Plummer's fumble for its own

**T**eam. By definition it involves a group that works together toward a common goal. If anything, this game—and the highlighted, clinching play—reflects this. Every man contributed along the way.

Pittsburgh struck first, as Steelers kicker Jeff Reed booted the initial score of the game through the uprights, a 47-yard field goal. It was symbolic of things to come, a foreshadowing that the sixth-seeded Pittsburgh football team had traveled to INVESCO Field at Mile High not only to play, but also to win. First blood: 3–zip at the end of quarter number one.

In the second quarter Pittsburgh wide receiver Cedrick Wilson pulled in a 12-yard pass from Ben Roethlisberger to put the next points on the board. Touchdown Steelers, and Reed punctuated that score with one more. Denver kicker Jason Elam managed a 23-yard field goal. Jerome Bettis then followed with a three-yard

This Steelers fan's sign says it all during the AFC Championship Game on January 22, 2006. Pittsburgh defeated the Denver Broncos 34–17 to advance to Super Bowl XL. *Getty Images*

touchdown run, his fumble against Indy the week prior (made on the same Counter 38 Power running play) now clearly just a bad memory. Reed hit the point after. This was starting to feel pretty good.

As if this well-rounded Steelers effort weren't enough, the ever-smiling Hines Ward caught a 17-yard pass from Big Ben seven seconds before the half ended, scoring six, and Reed added yet another point.

Not so fast. There was another half to play. The ebb and flow of an NFL game is broken into four quarters of well-planned play execution, and the Broncos would establish something more after halftime. Rallying, Denver's quarterback Jake Plummer saw that his toss to Ashley Lelie, a 30-yard reception, was on the playoff money. After the

**Some Keisel Facts**

Born in Provo, Utah, Brett Keisel attended Brigham Young University and was a seventh-round pick in the 2002 NFL draft. Of the seven college players taken by the Steelers in that draft, Keisel was the only one to make the final roster cut. Following defensive lineman Kimo von Oelhoffen's free-agency departure to the Jets, Keisel was installed as a starter on the front line.

Pittsburgh Steelers defensive end Brett Keisel came up big against the Denver Broncos during the 2005 NFL season's AFC Championship Game played on January 22, 2006.
*Getty Images*

Elam point after, the third quarter ended with the Broncos just 14 points behind Pittsburgh.

Ah, they couldn't catch up, right? Things were looking pretty good, but much can change in football with time still left on the clock.

Ever consistent, Reed nailed another sweet field-goal kick in the fourth quarter, this one for 42 yards. Pittsburgh Steelers fans viewing at home and those among the 76,775 people watching—diehards who had made the trip to Denver—could taste victory. Sure, the Steelers had the advantage at this point, but they needed to lock down the win.

Plummer had the ball and passed to Lelie for 38. Steelers defensive back Ike Taylor was called for a pass-interference penalty. Not good at all. Field position shifted in favor of Denver. Seizing the opportunity, running back Mike Anderson went three yards for the score. Pittsburgh

## WHAT IS COACHING?

Coaching is Bill Cowher removing the Steelers' regular-season performance from the board in the team's meeting room on December 5, 2005. Coaching a 7-5 team with three losses in a row demands focus to make the playoffs.

Coaching is being aware of the Pittsburgh Post-Gazette headline: "Is the Season Over?" after the most recent loss, the 38–31 regular-season game with Cincinnati.

Coaching is Cowher saying, "Clear your mind. Forget the past. Forget the future. Only one thing matters: Chicago. Every week's an elimination game now."

Coaching is focusing on game 13 that coming week, which the Steelers won 21-9 against the Bears, ending Chicago's eight-game winning streak.

Pittsburgh never lost another one that season, eight games all told, including the AFC championship against Denver, and especially the final one: the Super Bowl XL win.

That's coaching.

# Game Details

## Pittsburgh 34 • Denver 17

**Location:** INVESCO Field at Mile High Stadium, Denver, Colorado

**Attendance:** 76,775

**Box Score:**

| | | | | | |
|---|---|---|---|---|---|
| **Steelers** | 3 | 21 | 0 | 10 | **34** |
| **Broncos** | 0 | 3 | 7 | 7 | **17** |

*Scoring:*
PIT Reed 47-yard FG
PIT Wilson 12-yard pass from Roethlisberger (Reed PAT)
DEN Elam 23-yard FG
PIT Bettis 3-yard run (Reed PAT)
PIT Ward 17-yard pass from Roethlisberger (Reed PAT)
DEN Lelie 30-yard pass from Plummer (Elam PAT)
PIT Reed 42-yard FG
DEN Anderson 3-yard run (Elam PAT)
PIT Roethlisberger 4-yard run (Reed PAT)

| Team | FD | RUSH | A-C-I | PASS |
|---|---|---|---|---|
| **Steelers** | 20 | 33/90 | 29-21-0 | 268 |
| **Broncos** | 16 | 21/97 | 30-18-2 | 211 |

> The offense capitalized on every chance we had. Once we get a lead that big, the sharks are in the water. We keep coming.
>
> **—Steelers linebacker Joey Porter**

27, Denver 17. Ten points defined certain victory with 7:52 left. Members of Steelers Nation were feeling just a little uneasy at this point...

Enter the Pittsburgh defense: strong safety Troy Polamalu, trash-talking linebacker Joey Porter, and especially Brett Keisel, who racked up four tackles and two sacks in this game. The most important play of all, the clinching defensive play, involved Plummer holding the football and the Steelers wanting possession of it.

So what did the 6'5", 285-pound defensive end Keisel do? He dissed the Broncos line of defense. He tackled the Denver quarterback. He forced that prized pigskin free.

The Steelers recovered on the 17. Black and Gold fans could breathe a little now. Still, they'd been in this position the week before in Indianapolis. The Steelers needed a score.

Not to worry. Roethlisberger's four-yard, roll-left run sealed it, and Reed (10 total points in the game) drilled another. Denver's AFC championship bid was now out of reach, thanks to Keisel's key defensive stop.

All told, the Steelers' defense managed four turnovers to gain possession.

Linebacker Porter—ever the intimidator and game changer—had set up the first Pittsburgh touchdown when he smacked the ball free from the Denver quarterback's grasp. Casey Hampton recovered there on the Broncos' 39.

The Wilson touchdown catch followed not long after. Larry Foote and Taylor each plucked a Plummer interception along the way. Denver's running game ground to a halt with just 97 yards gained all day.

The early Steelers dominance would prove too much for the weary Broncos in the long run. Maybe the AFC divisional playoff game win against the New England Patriots (played a week and a day prior) had taken too much out of Denver. Then again, maybe Pittsburgh had a lot left in their tank.

This was a pure team effort with that we-not-me attitude, and the Keisel play clinched it.

# PITTSBURGH'S 14-SECOND SCORING FURY

Bradshaw's touchdown pass to Stallworth, a Denver fumble on the kickoff, a touchdown by Lynn Swann— Pittsburgh wins the 1978 AFC divisional playoff game

**I**f head coach Chuck Noll is to be known for one thing, other than winning Super Bowls, it's his ability to read potential talent. Noll's first NFL draft, 1969, included Notre Dame All-American quarterback Terry Hanratty, offensive lineman Jon Kolb, defensive end L.C. Greenwood, and defensive tackle Joe Greene, the Steelers' first-round choice that year. And that's just for starters.

In 1970, Pittsburgh picked defensive back Mel Blount and quarterback Terry Bradshaw.

In 1971, Frank Lewis, Jack Ham, Steve Davis, Gerry Mullins, Dwight White, Larry Brown, Ernie Holmes, and Mike Wagner became Steelers.

In 1972, Pittsburgh made Penn State University running back Franco Harris its first-round pick. That season the team posted an 11–3

Pittsburgh Steelers wide receivers John Stallworth (No. 82) and Lynn Swann (No. 88) pictured in August 1979 during summer training camp at St. Vincent College in Latrobe, Pennsylvania. *Getty Images*

record, made the playoffs, and Harris was involved in a little thing called the Immaculate Reception.

After a lackluster 1973 draft, the final pieces to the puzzle fell into place the following year. In the 1974 NFL draft, maybe the best for pure talent, the Steelers chose center Mike Webster (round five), linebacker Jack Lambert (round two), and their receiving duo of Lynn Swann (round one) and John Stallworth (round four).

Reread these names, and you'll count nine Hall of Famers among them—all players listed here from the 1974 draft were later inducted. By the 1978 playoff game against Denver, some were proven veterans, while others were just coming into their own. Two Steelers Super Bowl victories had preceded this divisional playoff game with the Broncos, and the third championship would soon follow. There's no question the Steelers were even better with Stallworth and Swann on the field— especially with the Steel Curtain defense to back up their offensive efforts.

## JOHN STALLWORTH

What can you say about a guy who played in six AFC championships and contributed to four Super Bowl wins? Oh yeah, and four Pro Bowls, too.

In 1984, as a veteran and NFL Comeback Player of the Year, Stallworth led the AFC with a career-high 1,395 yards on 80 receptions. Stallworth's career statistics from 1974 to 1987 numbered 537 receptions for 8,723 yards and 63 touchdowns.

In his 2002 Hall of Fame acceptance speech Stallworth said, "I've learned from the guys I played with in Pittsburgh and in college.... From Chuck Noll I've learned the meaning of true leadership. One aspect of that is to deny personal fame and glory for the sake of the team."

Durable, reliable, fluid on the field, and a true team player, he'll be remembered as the other half of Pittsburgh's balanced passing attack during the 1970s and beyond.

Franchise lore suggests that before the game, Pittsburgh's 6′6″ and 245-pound defensive end Greenwood sauntered intentionally close to some Broncos engaged in pregame warm-ups. He held an orange in his hands, symbolic of "the Orange Crush," the Broncos' nickname for their defense, derived from the popular soft drink. As a welcoming gesture, he crushed the fruit against the nearest Three Rivers Stadium wall.

# Game Details

## Pittsburgh 33 • Denver 10

**Location:** Three Rivers Stadium, Pittsburgh, Pennsylvania

**Attendance:** 48,921

**Box Score:**

| | | | | | |
|---|---|---|---|---|---|
| **Broncos** | 3 | 7 | 0 | 0 | **10** |
| **Steelers** | 6 | 13 | 0 | 14 | **33** |

*Scoring:*
DEN Turner 37-yard FG
PIT Harris 1-yard run (Gerela PAT failed)
PIT Harris 18-yard run (Gerela PAT)
PIT Gerela 24-yard FG
DEN Preston 3-yard run (Turner PAT)
PIT Gerela 27-yard FG
PIT Stallworth 45-yard pass from Bradshaw (Gerela PAT)
PIT Swann 38-yard pass from Bradshaw (Gerela PAT)

| Team | FD | RUSH | A-C-I | PASS |
|---|---|---|---|---|
| **Broncos** | 15 | 27/87 | 22-12-0 | 131 |
| **Steelers** | 24 | 40/153 | 29-16-1 | 272 |

After this pregame posturing and two quarters of play, the halftime score sat at Steelers 19, Broncos 10. It looked the same after a scoreless third quarter as well.

It was time for Pittsburgh to take control of the game.

No problem. In a span of just 14 fourth-quarter seconds, Bradshaw, who would complete 16 of 29 passes for 272 yards, threw a spiraling bomb to Stallworth for a 45-yard touchdown, a hoops-like jump ball caught in the end zone (one of his 10 receptions for 156 yards that day).

As luck would have it, Denver then muffed the kickoff, fumbling.

Regaining possession of the ball, the Steelers quickly capitalized as Bradshaw hit Swann for another satisfying reception, a leaping effort at the goal line that concluded with a kind of basket catch—if this were baseball—the reception going for 38 yards and a score.

## LYNN SWANN

Here's a trivia question for you to use someday: Who led the NFL with 577 punt-return yards his rookie year, a franchise record at the time?

The Steelers' No. 88, of course.

Swann was a three-time Pro Bowl player who played in four Pittsburgh Super Bowls. He was the MVP of Super Bowl X. His total of 364 Super Bowl receiving yards ranked number one at the time he retired. Swann was also named to the NFL's All-Decade Team of the 1970s. His career statistics for 1974–1982 included 336 receptions for 5,462 yards and 51 touchdowns.

In his 2001 Hall of Fame acceptance speech Swann said, "Now, I'm not here because I was that good. I'm here because of the people around me.... They made me that good. John Stallworth forced me to work. Going against Jack Ham in practice every day made me work.... These were the things that made our football team great."

His playing days included a flair for dramatic, gravity-defying catches, including the touchdown reception against Denver.

# A MORE POTENT PASSING GAME EMERGES

NFL owners met in March 1978, and what took place changed professional football, particularly in the realm of "rules of engagement."

Starting with the 1978 season, defensive backs had to cease contact with pass receivers five yards beyond the line of scrimmage. To enforce this, a side judge—ready, willing, and able to call an interference penalty—was added.

The potential of more Steelers scoring offense that coming season presented itself, and a high-flying passing game would emerge.

In the *Pittsburgh Press* that summer, Steelers quarterback Bradshaw said of the NFL ruling, "This is gonna stop all the people laying all over the receivers' backs. And that could definitely help me because a lot of times what has held us up is receivers getting jammed by a cornerback who is all over him."

Double trouble.

The second fourth-quarter pass reception and touchdown definitely iced the game. Both catches and scores happened so fast—framing the Broncos' kickoff fumble—that the entire sequence remains one classic sustained moment in Steelers history.

Both Roy Gerela point-after attempts were also good (he'd missed one on Pittsburgh's first score). The Steelers went up a decisive 33–10, crushing the Broncos. Harris cruised for 105 yards as well, and two touchdowns, as the Pittsburgh rushing and passing game created a two-headed, orange-eating monster that racked up 425 punishing yards of offense. The defense, including Greenwood, shut down Denver's offense the entire second half (no points).

It almost seemed too easy.

# HARBAUGH'S BOBBLED HAIL MARY

In the AFC Championship game, Colts quarterback Jim Harbaugh's end-zone-seeking bomb is broken up for an incompletion as time expires

**T**his dogged undertaking against the Indianapolis Colts put the Steelers in Super Bowl XXX. Defensive play dominated early, but as the game wound down, both offenses seemed destined to pull out a win. Each tried furiously to get it. For NFL fans, this postseason meeting included many great plays. The final play held more drama than some entire games.

Pittsburgh Steelers fans were eerily reminded of the 1994 AFC championship loss only a year before in the same Three Rivers Stadium location. That score: Chargers 17, Steelers 13. In that one, the Steelers drove to reach the San Diego 9-yard line. Good, right? Black and Gold hopes were dashed when Chargers linebacker Dennis Gibson knocked down Neil O'Donnell's fourth-down pass, which, if completed, would have won it for Pittsburgh.

Pittsburgh Steelers fans wave Terrible Towels during the AFC Championship Game against the Indianapolis Colts at Three Rivers Stadium on January 14, 1996. *Getty Images*

In the Indianapolis game, the outcome was positively reversed.

This one had the same feel to it, though. In the 1994 AFC championship, Pittsburgh was up 10–3 at the half. In the 1995 AFC Championship Game, Pittsburgh led 10–6.

A five-yard touchdown pass—O'Donnell to Kordell Stewart—put them ahead as the second quarter concluded. Again, there was that definite feeling that the team needed to step it up a bit. As Steelers head coach Bill Cowher later said on reflection, "I felt like we'd gone into that half and had very little to show for it."

The Colts sure weren't ready to lie down and lose this one.

Halftime was over, at least officially. The controversial first-half Stewart touchdown had provided lingering angst for Colts fans, as some of them would argue it shouldn't have counted. Clearly televised replays showed Stewart's white shoes with black laces stepping out of bounds in the end zone, making him ineligible for the catch. The referee saw it otherwise.

Still earlier in the first half, Indy's defensive back Jason Belser (the same defender on the Steelers' first-half touchdown reception) had caught a break too. Back then he'd slammed Stewart with a blatant pass interference move at the goal line—the incomplete pass had touchdown written all over it.

Things were evened up now.

Fast-forward to the third quarter. Right out of the locker room and no doubt inspired by some second-half planning, Jim Harbaugh staged a downfield passing drive with the exuberance of a kid playing Pop Warner football—61 yards in nine plays. But the Pittsburgh defense stepped up, as it so often had in this game, and held the Colts. The Colts settled for a field goal: Steelers 10, Colts 9.

After this, the Steelers' ground game, like an aging pickup truck on a cold winter day, failed to get going. Three tries and out, the Black and Gold defense was back on the field. Nine plays later the Colts tried for a field goal, which drifted wide.

Next, Pittsburgh extended the lead to 13–9 on a Norm Johnson field goal. Then with the fourth quarter lingering at the 10:57 mark, Johnson would whiff on another three-point attempt.

Who would win this game?

Want attitude? Steelers linebacker Greg Lloyd (6'2", 228 pounds) later said of Harbaugh's game dramatics, "Nobody on our defense feared him." And you know what? Pittsburgh's play on the field pretty much matched that statement—right to the wire if you discount the next big play that Indy and their quarterback dished out.

Gliding downfield into the corner, the Colts' Floyd Turner worked himself free. Harbaugh simultaneously eluded the Steelers blitz and threw a rainbow to his receiver for a 47-yard touchdown. Time: 8:46. Score: Colts 16, Steelers 13.

# Game Details

## Pittsburgh 20 • Indianapolis 16

**Location:** Three Rivers Stadium, Pittsburgh, Pennsylvania

**Attendance:** 61,062

**Box Score:**

| | | | | | |
|---|---|---|---|---|---|
| **Colts** | 3 | 3 | 3 | 7 | **16** |
| **Steelers** | 3 | 7 | 3 | 7 | **20** |

*Scoring:*
IND Blanchard 34-yard FG
PIT N. Johnson 31-yard FG
IND Blanchard 36-yard FG
PIT Stewart 5-yard pass from O'Donnell (N. Johnson PAT)
IND Blanchard 37-yard FG
PIT N. Johnson 36-yard FG
IND Turner 47-yard pass from Harbaugh (Blanchard PAT)
PIT Morris 1-yard run (N. Johnson PAT)

| Team | FD | RUSH | A-C-I | PASS |
|---|---|---|---|---|
| **Colts** | 16 | 23/83 | 34-21-0 | 245 |
| **Steelers** | 21 | 24/80 | 41-25-1 | 205 |

> It seemed like it took forever. You could just see this big ball. It looked huge, and it looked like it was coming in slow motion.
>
> **—Darren Perry, Steelers safety, on Jim Harbaugh's Hail Mary attempt**

# THE HAIL MARY PASS

This forward pass, which can pay high dividends or yield low returns, is an act of desperation with a dash of hope thrown in. It's almost always a long bomb. It usually comes at the end of the half and most memorably at the end of a game, with few seconds left.

Since the name of the play invokes the Roman Catholic prayer to the Virgin Mary, it's called and executed based on the playbook's designations and maybe sometimes with a reverent petition and fervent request added to it.

As a play, it includes three, four, or five wide receivers spreading the defense with their pass routes downfield.

Even if the intended receiver doesn't catch the ball, and it might be several "intended receivers" in some instances, the offense may draw a pass-interference penalty for their effort. If pass interference is called on the last play of the game, the offense will be able to run yet one more play because the game can't end on a defensive penalty.

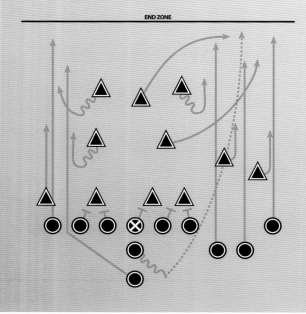

To defend this wish-and-a-prayer pass effort, the defense establishes zone coverage—that is, until the ball is lofted downfield.

The Immaculate Reception, Terry Bradshaw's pass as the Steelers faced fourth-and-10 from their own 40 with just 22 seconds left and with Pittsburgh trailing the Oakland Raiders by the score of 7–6, is certainly the most famous example in franchise history. The thwarted Harbaugh effort ranks right behind it as the Hail Mary pass in Steelers history goes.

Colts quarterback Jim Harbaugh, pictured here during the 1995 AFC Championship Game, nearly pulled off a dramatic last-second win with his Hail Mary toss to receiver Aaron Bailey. *Getty Images*

If Lloyd wasn't fearful, surely some members of Steelers Nation were. The on-field drama increased steadily.

Pittsburgh reached the 50 but couldn't convert. They punted to Indy. Time: 6:29 to go. The Colts fumbled on the next play as running back Lamont Warren lost control of the ball, but Indianapolis guard Joe Staysniak looked the pigskin into his hands like a receiver and held it.

And sometimes blown plays—the next one on defense, in particular—actually yield good results.

Warren ran left after a Harbaugh handoff. Steelers defensive back Myron Bell, who was supposed to blitz, did not. Cornerback Willie Williams adjusted, streaking in from the other side. His momentum gave him just enough reach to take down Warren—by the ankles. Beyond the ball carrier, the field was wide open.

Whew.

Thwarted, the Colts punted. Andre Hastings took it 12 yards. At the 33, and with 3:03 to go, O'Donnell started a drive. He hit Slash Stewart for 13. John L. Williams caught one for seven.

Then the Steelers dodged a bullet.

A pass intended for Mills was perfectly thrown—to Indy linebacker Quentin Coryatt, who dropped it when Mills swatted at him.

Tell me you weren't pacing then, Steelers fan.

Then with fourth-and-three, O'Donnell somehow hit Hastings for a first down. Then he passed long to Mills, throwing a strike to his outside shoulder for 37 yards deep inside the red zone. Bam Morris went one yard into the end zone for the score. Johnson's point after added another: Steelers 20, Colts 16.

But wait, Harbaugh somehow had the ball again, with enough time to stage his own little rally. A field goal wouldn't matter because they were down four. A touchdown would win it. All the while Steelers fans in the stands bounced up and down as if they were at a rock concert.

Mr. Comeback, Harbaugh, staged a drive, passing downfield and running to midfield, ignoring failed efforts, whatever he had to do. With second-and-two, the Steelers nearly intercepted. With third-and-two, the Colts failed to complete another pass. With fourth-and-two, Harbaugh hit his man, wide receiver Sean Dawkins.

Would the clock ever run out? The Colts were now 38 yards from the goal line, first-and-10 with 21 seconds to go. Harbaugh, in shotgun formation, felt Steelers defensive pressure waiting like sharks in the water, but the Colts quarterback slipped away and scrambled to the 28. He took the snap and spiked the ball to the turf, stopping the time: five seconds to go.

He had to be thinking, "We can win this thing."

The play, your basic Hail Mary, had three Colts receivers set to the same side. All knew their responsibility—go deep, catch the ball if you can. Harbaugh dropped back to pass and lofted the pigskin. Aaron Bailey, the intended receiver, had the arcing ball land right where Harbaugh tried to put it. In. His. Hands.

Five Steelers defenders, including defensive back Randy Fuller, surrounded Bailey, who caught the ball—oh so briefly in reality but so long as you watched the final play—then lost control of it. Still, the call was close enough that many Colts had their arms in the air to signal a touchdown, including their quarterback.

Incomplete!

Some folks hang horseshoes for luck. Those who wear them on their helmets could have used some. The Steelers were going to the Super Bowl for the fifth time in franchise history.

# HARRIS'S NINE YARDS TOWARD MVP

Game MVP Franco Harris matched a strong defensive effort with a third-quarter nine-yard scoring run—Pittsburgh's first Super Bowl touchdown ever

**P**ittsburgh Steelers players on the field that day credit their head coach Chuck Noll with creating a relaxed but ready attitude heading into Super Bowl IX against the Minnesota Vikings. Noll had some previous experience with the territory and how to handle the pressure—or rather, how not to. His first visit to the big game came not on the Pittsburgh sideline but as a Baltimore Colts assistant coach. Their opponent in Super Bowl III, the New York Jets, took that game in an upset NFL fans well remember. A relaxed but effective Joe Namath played an important role in the victory.

Yes, that was the same Namath—the poolside, pregame quarterback—who had predicted a Jets win prior to the AFL-NFL "interleague championship" kickoff at the Orange Bowl in Miami: "I've got news for you. We're gonna win

Steelers running back Franco Harris, carrying the ball during the January 12, 1975, game, scored the first Super Bowl touchdown in franchise history. *Getty Images*

# FRANCO FACTS

Born in Fort Dix, New Jersey, to an African American father and Italian American mother, Franco Harris attended Penn State University and played for the Nittany Lions under head coach Joe Paterno.

The Steelers selected the big running back (6'2" and 230 pounds) first in the 1972 NFL draft, the 13th player taken overall that year. In 1972 he was named NFL Offensive Rookie of the Year.

Harris played 13 NFL seasons (1972–1984), a dozen with Pittsburgh, before finishing out his career with the Seattle Seahawks. He still considers himself a Steelers fan.

Harris's Italian Army established itself as a homegrown brand of Three Rivers Stadium fan that wore army helmets with Harris's No. 32 on them during the 1970s and early 1980s.

During those 13 years, he rushed 2,949 times for 12,120 total yards and 91 touchdowns, including the big score in Super Bowl IX. Harris also carried the ball for more than 1,000 yards in eight different seasons, including his first and last with Pittsburgh.

His 100-yard rushing games total 47. As a pass receiver, he caught 307 for 2,287 yards and nine touchdowns. Harris averaged 4.1 running yards per carry and 7.4 passing yards per catch during his career.

He played in five AFC championships, sitting out another because of injury, and four Super Bowls, all victories. In 19 postseason games, Harris had 1,556 rushing yards and 17 touchdowns.

Named the MVP of Super Bowl IX, his 354 total rushing yards and 24 Super Bowl points in four games established records.

A nine-time Pro Bowl player, Harris is on the NFL 1970s All-Decade Team. Harris is also a member of the 1990 Pro Football Hall of Fame class. His Steelers No. 32 is unofficially retired.

the game. I guarantee it." And they did. (The Colts were favored by a 19-point spread, mind you.)

Maybe there was something to that calm and confident approach.

As Steelers linebacker Andy Russell has related, Noll encouraged his players to relax this time. "Go out, no bed check, get this town [New Orleans] out of your system," their head coach told them.

# Game Details

## Pittsburgh 16 • Minnesota 6

**Location:** Tulane Stadium, New Orleans, Louisiana

**Attendance:** 80,997

**Box Score:**

| | | | | | |
|---|---|---|---|---|---|
| **Steelers** | 0 | 2 | 7 | 7 | **16** |
| **Vikings** | 0 | 0 | 0 | 6 | **6** |

*Scoring:*

PIT White safety on Tarkenton in end zone

PIT Harris 9-yard run (Gerela PAT)

MIN T. Brown recovered blocked punt in end zone (Cox PAT failed)

PIT L. Brown 4-yard pass from Bradshaw (Gerela PAT)

| Team | FD | RUSH | A-C-I | PASS |
|---|---|---|---|---|
| **Steelers** | 17 | 57/249 | 14–9–0 | 84 |
| **Vikings** | 9 | 21/17 | 26–11–3 | 102 |

> Whatever it takes.
>
> **—A frequent Chuck Noll phrase uttered before, during, and after games**

Franco Harris has stressed the importance of this attitude as well, saying, "The way Chuck approached it made all the difference in the world."

In some ways this Super Bowl was won the week before it began. Still, they play the games for a reason. Pittsburgh had put two points on

## NOLL KNEW TALENT

In 1972 Nittany Lions All-American running back Lydell Mitchell was the guy. The man. A sure-bet NFL draft choice to be. Mitchell's college teammate Franco Harris was solid too, especially as a blocking back.

Picking Mitchell over Harris in the 1972 NFL draft was a no-brainer for many. The media figured as much. They thought the Steelers surely would. Not head coach Chuck Noll, though. He'd gone against popular belief before, selecting Joe Greene first in 1969, for instance, and his draft-based approach to building a dynasty team would prove many wrong in the long run.

Taking Harris as the Steelers first-round pick in 1972 (and the 13th player overall) was no exception. Mitchell would indeed gain entrance into the NFL, but only as a Baltimore Colts second-round selection and 48th player overall.

While Mitchell would go on to have a decent NFL career—three consecutive 1,000-yard seasons (1975–1977), Pro Bowl status, and three AFC East division titles with the Colts—many fans would have to say the Steelers made the right choice.

True enough, Mitchell also led the NFL in pass receptions twice (1974 with 72 catches; 1977 with 71 receptions). He was a good ballplayer. Who knows what the Steelers would have done with him on the roster.

The thing is, Noll somehow knew what Pittsburgh could do without Mitchell, and with Harris in a Black and Gold jersey.

the board in the first half (Steelers 2, Vikings 0) and needed to establish command of the game after halftime. But first Pittsburgh had to get the ball. It didn't take long. The Vikings muffed the second-half kickoff as Bill Brown fumbled and Pittsburgh's Marv Kellum claimed it.

The Steelers soon scored.

On his nine-yard run for a touchdown, Harris took the handoff from Terry Bradshaw and flowed left with his typical casual yet powerful grace untouched and into the end zone for the first Steelers Super Bowl touchdown in franchise history—and what would turn out to be the only rushing points of the game. Roy Gerela hit the extra point. The score heading into the fourth quarter: Steelers 9, Vikings 0.

Then disaster happened—or at least the threat of it. With a nine-point lead moving toward their first Super Bowl victory, the Steelers' Bobby Walden attempted to punt. The Vikings' Matt Blair blocked it. Terry Brown recovered the ball for a touchdown.

Minnesota's point-after attempt failed, a relief to those of us watching, as every point counted in this one. With the Steel Curtain in the process of limiting Minnesota to just 119 total yards, victory almost seemed assured. Right?

To clinch it, Bradshaw rolled right, eluded a defender, and pitched a fastball and strike to receiver Larry Brown—a four-yard completion for a touchdown. Brown caught three passes for 49 yards on the day (his longest going for 20). Kicker Gerela made it Steelers 16, Vikings 6, with his point after.

Despite field conditions and underdog status, Pittsburgh dominated.

Harris's 158 yards on 34 carries established a Super Bowl rushing record. Rocky Bleier added 65 more on 17 tries—his longest went for 18 yards. Even Bradshaw ran five times for 33 yards, with one stretching to 17.

And what of the famed Purple People Eaters, the Vikings famed defensive line? They were no-shows this day.

# HAM'S INTERCEPTION PAVES THE WAY

The 1974 AFC Championship Game was tied, 10–10, when Jack Ham provided a crucial momentum shift

A defensive adjustment—simple but oh so effective—developed by defensive tackle Joe Greene, defensive coach Bud Carson, and the other Steelers defenders during the 1974 regular season, galvanized the front four's onslaught. In short, this move, called the Stunt 4-3, saw Greene shift his position into the gap between the offensive guard and center before the snap. Once established there, he would tilt his considerable body (6'4" and 275 pounds) at an appropriate angle, just as a predator regards it prey before moving in for the kill.

What did the Stunt 4–3 do? It made opposing quarterbacks uncomfortable on the pass rush, not to mention simple running plays. It often drew double-team blocking on Greene, freeing up other members of the Steel Curtain line to do their damage; often, Greene still made the play. It

Pittsburgh Steelers linebacker Jack Ham stands on the sideline during the 1974 AFC Championship Game against the Oakland Raiders at Oakland-Alameda County Coliseum. His crucial interception helped the Steelers defeat the Raiders 24–13. *Getty Images*

also freed up Pittsburgh linebackers to defend the midrange pass and, ideally, intercept the ball.

Like all postseason teams in any given year, the aim is to win each game. The ultimate quest is a Super Bowl appearance and victory. The Oakland Raiders were no different. The defending World Champion Miami Dolphins—who prevailed as AFC Champions the past three years as well, and won the last two Super Bowls—were also certainly in the mix.

# Game Details

## Pittsburgh 24 • Oakland 13

**Location:** Oakland-Alameda County Coliseum, Oakland, California

**Attendance:** 53,515

**Box Score:**

| | | | | | |
|---|---|---|---|---|---|
| **Steelers** | 0 | 3 | 0 | 21 | **24** |
| **Raiders** | 3 | 0 | 7 | 3 | **13** |

*Scoring:*
OAK Blanda 40-yard FG
PIT Gerela 23-yard FG
OAK Branch 38-yard pass from Stabler (Blanda PAT)
PIT Harris 8-yard run (Gerela PAT)
PIT Swann 6-yard pass from Bradshaw (Gerela PAT)
OAK Blanda 24-yard FG
PIT Harris 21-yard run (Gerela PAT)

| Team | FD | RUSH | A-C-I | PASS |
|---|---|---|---|---|
| **Steelers** | 20 | 50/224 | 17-8-1 | 95 |
| **Raiders** | 15 | 21/29 | 36-19-3 | 249 |

"Dobre Shunka" is the Polish and Slovak phrase for "Good Ham." Here Pittsburgh fans display a classic Steelers dynasty-era sign during the last game played at Three Rivers Stadium on December 16, 2000. *Getty Images*

The truth is, many fans and the media felt one of these two teams (and not the Steelers) would win the Super Bowl this year. In the end, neither team would even make it to the game.

In the much-hyped (and deservedly so) 1974 AFC divisional championship between the Raiders and Dolphins, Oakland quarterback Ken Stabler executed his fourth touchdown of the California December day, a triple-teamed Clarence Davis eight-yard catch with 26 seconds remaining. Dubbed the "Sea of Hands" in NFL history lore, the 28–26 Oakland win ensured a meeting with Pittsburgh in the AFC championship.

One of the greatest plays in the Raiders' franchise history? No doubt about it.

Prior to that Oakland-Miami matchup, Raiders head coach John Madden had implied to the media that these were the best two teams in football. And why not? Almost everyone else said the same thing—except for the Steelers fans and franchise.

After the Raiders' thrilling AFC divisional win, Pittsburgh head coach Chuck Noll had other news for his Black and Gold players. Quoting Noll in the NFL Films America's Game series, Greene said, "The best team in the NFL didn't play yesterday. The best football team is sitting right here in this room."

And with that motivational attitude, the Steelers entered into a game they weren't supposed to win.

After one quarter of Oakland-Alameda County Coliseum football, the Raiders held a 3–0 lead on a 40-yard George Blanda field goal. After two quarters, the Steelers had tied it with a 23-yard Roy Gerela kick. In

## JACK HAM FACTS

Born in Johnstown, Pennsylvania, on December 23, 1948, Jack Ham was a homegrown linebacker and an important part of the 1970s and early 1980s Steelers legacy.

The 6'1" and 225-pound Keystone State native attended Pennsylvania State University and played for Joe Paterno, who presented Ham at the linebacker's 1988 NFL Pro Football Hall of Fame induction.

Pittsburgh took him in the second round of the 1971 NFL draft. He was the 34th player selected. Ham played a dozen years in the NFL (1971–1982), all with the Steelers, and he owns four Super Bowl rings. His NFL career included 32 interceptions, 25½ sacks, and 21 fumble recoveries off opponents. Ham played in eight consecutive Pro Bowls.

His Three Rivers Stadium fan-generated nickname during his playing days, Dobre Shunka, is Polish for "good ham."

Ham may be best known for his ability to read offensive plays before or as they happened and his talent to defend effectively.

the third quarter, Stabler hit Cliff Branch for 38 yards and a touchdown. Blanda booted in the point after, establishing the score at 10–3, with the Raiders leading heading into the fourth quarter.

The Steelers struck next, early on, and with deliberate dominance.

On a simple draw up the middle, a determined Franco Harris took the handoff from Terry Bradshaw and bulled his way on an eight-yard run for the touchdown, rolling into the end zone with his hands and arms wrapped firmly around the ball. Following Gerela's point after, the score was tied.

Oakland had the ball and was prepared to put on a drive. Stabler took the snap from No. 00, Jim Otto, their Hall of Fame center playing in his last season of 15, all of which had been with Oakland. The Black and Silver Raiders offensive line clashed with the Black and Gold Steelers front four.

From the pocket, the southpaw Stabler wheeled and threw to his right just as three Steelers defenders pressured him, intending to put the pass into running back Charlie Smith's hands. Pittsburgh linebacker Jack Ham clearly read the move. Anticipating the throw, he stepped up to make the interception and return the ball in the direction of the Steelers' end zone: a crucial turnover for certain.

The wheels were in motion.

After Ham's interception, Bradshaw delivered a six-yard touchdown pass to Lynn Swann, and Gerela kicked the point after. Oakland's Blanda would drill a 24-yard field goal. Pittsburgh's Harris would score his second touchdown of the game in the last minute, earning 21 of his 111 yards on the day with 29 attempts. Rocky Bleier would carry for 98 more yards on 18 touches, his longest going for 23 yards.

As for the Raiders and their rushing totals, Clarence Davis, who had caught the "Sea of Hands" game-winning pass the playoff game before this, and Oakland's Pete Banaszak only moved the ball a total of 29 yards all day.

The Steelers' first conference championship was at hand.

# THE GREATEST INTERCEPTION NEVER MADE

At a crucial point in an AFC divisional playoff game versus the Indianapolis Colts, safety Troy Polamalu's apparent interception was overturned on further review

**T**he agony. The ecstasy. Sometimes you have to wonder why Steelers fans put up with this.

Quarterback Ben Roethlisberger and his Pittsburgh offense seized control early on, passing on the Colts' secondary, moving the ball downfield at will. They went up 14–0 with 3:56 to go in the first quarter. This wasn't so much looking like a playoff game as it was a clinic on well-executed NFL football. A play-action pass here and simple slant route there, Big Ben roamed the backfield, holding in the pocket, hitting his receivers Hines Ward and Heath Miller with smooth aplomb. His poise seemed contagious.

The Steelers' swarming defense matched its offensive effort, punishing Peyton Manning the same way the New York Giants' defensive line did the New England Patriots and Tom Brady in

Pittsburgh Steelers defensive back Troy Polamalu, No. 43, holding the ball while celebrating his interception off Colts quarterback Peyton Manning—an overturned call when officials ruled the ball incomplete after a replay challenge. The next day the NFL indicated the interception reversal had been wrong. *Getty Images*

Super Bowl XLII. Linebacker Joey Porter's trash-talking and overall exuberance could be seen on the field and Pittsburgh sideline for anyone looking on. It was fun. But the game wasn't over yet. Yes, the Steelers controlled much of it. The last quarter, however, played out like an entirely different game.

Let's fast-forward to the fourth quarter, 5:33 to go, with the score Steelers 21, Colts 10, and the Super Bowl favorites in their blue and white uniforms holding possession of the ball.

Manning took the snap, dropped back in his well-protected pocket, and passed the ball, swiftly throwing it over the middle. Troy Polamalu stepped in and grabbed the fastball while moving right over the 50-yard line and the painted Colts helmet on the midfield's playing surface. Linebacker Porter—who always seemed to be in on making or shadowing plays during this game—also converged.

Polamalu moved so fast to intercept that he caught the ball then flopped forward, his right hand bracing his body, his left hand and arm cradling the prize, his long black hair trailing out of his helmet as an afterthought. No. 43 rolled, holding the ball, then stood in one motion—and somehow the pigskin, as if possessed with a mind of its own, flipped out of his grasp.

Had he held it long enough?

That would be resolved shortly, but for now the Steelers' defensive back fell on the fumble, recovering it on the 49-yard line, holding it safely on the turf's big painted P, of NFL Playoffs.

A huge postseason play, for sure.

The nearby official signaled the interception, and Polamalu—still in possession of the ball—ran off the field in celebration.

But wait.

The Colts challenged the call, the interception, and possibly the game-clinching play, one of the biggest in Steelers football history.

And then came the ruling on the field: "After reviewing the play, the defender caught the ball, lost it prior to getting his knee off the ground, therefore it is an incomplete pass." Overruled if you will. Nullified. Reversed.

Robbed. Replays refuted the referee's call.

# Game Details

## Pittsburgh 21 • Indianapolis 18

**Location:** RCA Dome, Indianapolis, Indiana

**Attendance:** 57,449

**Box Score:**

| | | | | | |
|---|---|---|---|---|---|
| **Steelers** | 14 | 0 | 7 | 0 | **21** |
| **Colts** | 0 | 3 | 0 | 15 | **18** |

*Scoring:*

PIT Randle El 6-yard pass from Roethlisberger (Reed PAT)
PIT Miller 7-yard pass from Roethlisberger (Reed PAT)
IND Vanderjagt 20-yard FG
PIT Bettis 1-yard run (Reed PAT)
IND Clark 50-yard pass from Manning (Vanderjagt PAT)
IND James 3-yard run (Wayne pass from Manning)

| Team | FD | RUSH | A-C-I | PASS |
|---|---|---|---|---|
| **Steelers** | 21 | 42/112 | 24-14-1 | 183 |
| **Colts** | 15 | 14/58 | 38-22-0 | 247 |

> Right when I thought it was over it really wasn't.
>
> **—Pittsburgh linebacker Joey Porter**

# INTERCEPTION DENIED

It's a cool footnote to an epic playoff game filled with bizarre plays. Troy Polamalu made a great play for an interception, which was incorrectly reversed by referee Pete Morelli.

On a first-and-20 at the Colts's 44-yard line with less than six minutes left in the game, Indianapolis Colts quarterback Peyton Manning threw a pass intended for tight end Bryan Fletcher (81). But Polamalu (43) streaked across the field to jump the route and intercept it. After Polamalu did so, linebacker Joey Porter blocked Fletcher, preventing him from tackling the safety.

Polamalu was touched down at the Steelers's 48, fumbled, and then recovered again at the 48. After the call was challenged and inexplicably reversed, Edgerrin James scored a three-yard touchdown to pull the Colts within three.

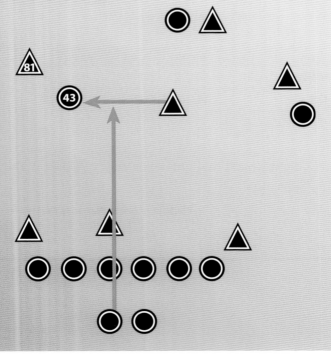

Bad call or not, the Colts scored four plays later and boosted the score with a two-point conversion. Score: Steelers 21, Colts 18.

The game wasn't over just yet. Pittsburgh Steelers fans everywhere felt sick, victimized, angry, and dismayed all at once.

Porter later said that he was so mad on the field he couldn't even talk—uncommon for the loquacious linebacker. The Colts had the ball again. He responded to the frustration with one Manning sack, then another to squelch any remaining Indy momentum.

"Cheat that," Porter barked on the sidelines for all to hear. "Cheat that."

Observers were calling it Pittsburgh's game at that point. In retrospect, Steelers fans should have known better.

Late in the fourth quarter, on a play that would likely seal victory, a usually sure-handed Bettis fumbled at the goal line. The Colts' Nick Harper recovered it.

Big Ben traded offense for defense, dropping back after the recovery like a linebacker in zone coverage. Roethlisberger shoestring tackled the Indy player as he ran downfield with the ball for the certain winning score.

Mike Vanderjagt, the most accurate field-goal kicker in the NFL, then booted the potentially game-tying 46-yarder wide right.

In the end, and in a fourth quarter filled with memorable plays, the Colts nearly won it.

The next day the NFL indicated the reversal on Polamalu's interception had been wrong.

# MADDOX RALLIES TO WIN WILD-CARD GAME

Tommy Maddox leads Pittsburgh back from a 24–7 third-quarter deficit in a dramatic AFC wild-card win against the Browns

**T**his was easily one of the most dramatic comeback victories in franchise playoff history. If you turned the television off in the third quarter, too bad: you missed witnessing all that we love about the NFL and the Pittsburgh Steelers. Down, but not out. Here you had a professional football journeyman playing the game of his life. Maddox's own career story was just as amazing.

A first-round NFL draft choice out of the University of California at Los Angeles (1992), he'd worn a Denver Broncos uniform (1992–1993), the colors of the Los Angeles Rams (1994), the New York Giants (1995), and even the Atlanta Falcons before he was released in the 1997 preseason. For a time, he sold insurance.

His love of the game brought him back to play for the Arena Football League's New Jersey

Up 33–21 with just over 10 minutes to play, Cleveland surely looked like they had the 2002 AFC wild card playoff game in hand. Unhesitatingly, Maddox pulled the Steelers back into game-winning range. His calm, steady control made the winning touchdown play—with 54 seconds left—possible. *Getty Images*

Red Dogs (2000) and the Xtreme Football League's Los Angeles Xtreme (2001). By then his player equity was rising again, though mostly through offbeat pop culture notice: he'd been named MVP of the XFL, which folded after just one season. He joined the Steelers in 2001, and in the next several years established himself as one of the top quarterbacks in the NFL.

In 2002 Maddox had helped quarterback his team to a 10–5–1 record, tops in the AFC North. Before 62,595 Heinz Field fans, he was

## TOMMY MADDOX FACTS

- Played five seasons with the Steelers (2001–2005).
- Passed for 234 completions on 377 attempts (62.1 percent) during the 2002 season, totaling 2,836 yards for his quarterbacking efforts and 20 touchdowns.
- In 2003 Maddox threw for 298 completions on 519 attempts (57.4 percent). Total yards: 3,414 and 18 touchdowns.
- He owns a Super Bowl XL ring and retired after the 2005 season.

trying to do the near-impossible: claw his way out of a fourth-quarter playoff hole.

Up 7–0 in the first quarter and 17–7 by the half, Cleveland's quarterback, Kelly Holcomb, starting in place of the injured Tim Couch, controlled the game with short runs and dramatic passes.

It got worse for Pittsburgh before it got better.

After the break the Steelers went down 24–7 on a 15-yard touchdown pass from Holcomb to wideout Dennis Northcutt. Pittsburgh fought back, though, with a six-yard scoring pass from Maddox to Plaxico Burress—no, he wasn't always with the New York Super Bowl Giants. At the end of three quarters of play, the Browns held a 24–14 lead.

The NFL's 2002 Comeback Player of the Year was about to earn that reputation. Literally. Up 33–21 with a little more than 10 minutes to play, Cleveland surely looked like it had the playoff game in hand. Unhesitatingly, Maddox pulled the Steelers back into game-winning range.

In the fourth quarter, he hit tight end Jerame Tuman for a three-yard touchdown pass completion. Cleveland followed with a 22-yard pass to André Davis from Holcomb for the score. The two-point conversion attempt, a pass, failed—the score stood at 33–21 with the Browns still in the lead.

# Game Details

## Pittsburgh 36 • Cleveland 33

**Location:** Heinz Field, Pittsburgh, Pennsylvania

**Attendance:** 62,595

**Box Score:**

| | | | | | |
|---|---|---|---|---|---|
| **Browns** | 7 | 10 | 7 | 9 | **33** |
| **Steelers** | 0 | 7 | 7 | 22 | **36** |

*Scoring:*
CLE Green 1-yard run (Dawson PAT)
CLE Northcutt 32-yard pass from Holcomb (Dawson PAT)
PIT Randle El 66-yard punt return (Reed PAT)
CLE Dawson 31-yard FG
CLE Northcutt 15-yard pass from Holcomb (Dawson PAT)
PIT Burress 6-yard pass from Maddox (Reed PAT)
CLE Dawson 24-yard FG
PIT Tuman 3-yard pass from Maddox (Reed PAT)
CLE A. Davis 22-yard pass from Holcomb (Holcomb pass to Morgan failed)
PIT Ward 5-yard pass from Maddox (Reed PAT)
PIT Fuamatu-Ma'afala 3-yard run (Tuman pass from Randle El good for 2 points)

| Team | FD | RUSH | A-C-I | PASS |
|---|---|---|---|---|
| **Browns** | 21 | 28/38 | 43-26-1 | 409 |
| **Steelers** | 30 | 20/89 | 48-30-2 | 343 |

# PITTSBURGH STEELERS NFL COMEBACK PLAYERS OF THE YEAR

Selected by the Associated Press since 1972.

**1984**  John Stallworth

**1996**  Jerome Bettis

**2002**  Tommy Maddox

Maddox wasn't done just yet. His 77-yard Elway-esque drive culminated with a five-yard pass to Hines Ward with just 3:06 remaining. Jeff Reed nailed the point after. Score: 33–28. Maybe they could pull this thing out after all.

Could Holcomb and the Browns run the game clock out? That thought was on the minds of every Steelers fan watching. Answer: no.

After a failed third-and-12 Cleveland effort with receiver Northcutt dropping an easy pass (mercy!), the Browns punted.

In succession, smelling a come-from-behind win in the making, Maddox passed to Burress for 24 yards. He completed one to Hines Ward for 10 more. He hit Burress for another 17, then Ward for seven more.

Could you believe it? Now within goal-line striking distance, running back Chris Fuamatu-Ma'afala thundered right up the middle on a three-yard run for the winning touchdown.

Maddox's calm, steady control made the winning touchdown play with 54 seconds left possible.

Holcomb—who completed a last-ditch 16-yard pass to wide receiver Andre King (not Davis this time) in field-goal range as the clock ran out—threw for 429 yards passing in the losing effort, and Kevin Johnson claimed 140 of them.

Maddox put up 367 yards on the winning side, as Ward posted 104, while Burress pulled in 100 more.

In the 2002 AFC divisional playoff road game to follow, the Steelers and Maddox would turn 20 points off three Tennessee Titans turnovers. This one had all the twists and turns of the Cleveland wild-card game. At the end of regulation the score would be tied at 31, as Titans kicker Joe Nedney whiffed on a field-goal try that could have won the thing at the end of regulation play—and yet again in overtime, when he missed the second chance at the game winner. After the two failed tries, Nedney—one of the biggest kickers ever to play NFL football at 6'5" and 225 pounds—wouldn't miss yet another redemptive field-goal attempt.

Tommy brought the whole team together at halftime and told us what we were going to do. He said: "If you don't think we're going to win this game, you need to go back into the locker room."

**—Pittsburgh Steelers wideout Terance Mathis**

# WILLIE PARKER'S RECORD RUN

The longest running play in Super Bowl history, 75 yards, offered leverage in a game that threatened to go either way

**A**s a Steelers fan, you had to love it. Pittsburgh's running back Jerome Bettis, now returning to his hometown of Detroit, Michigan, after 13 memorable NFL years, ran out onto the field first, before the rest of the players—at linebacker Joey Porter and the team's collective request, observers later learned.

It gave you goosebumps. Made you a little teary.

This may have been an away-game location, but Terrible Towels exuberantly waved in the stands. Many of the 68,206 people packing Ford Field demonstrated their love for the Black and Gold. Pregame excitement and support were great, but there was a Super Bowl game still to be played.

Remember now, the Steelers had a hill to climb as they attempted to do what had never been done before: win three road playoff games and then the NFL's Vince Lombardi Trophy. The

From a fan's perspective, Willie Parker's acceleration on the 75-yard record Super Bowl run and touchdown defied physical properties, as everyone else on the field seemed to move in slow motion. *Getty Images*

challenge would be even tougher against the league's highest scoring offense, the Seattle Seahawks.

After a first half that demonstrated some tentative, awkward, and even blundering plays, the score stood at 7–3, with the Steelers in the lead.

The second quarter was highlighted with a third-and-28 completion from Pittsburgh quarterback Ben Roethlisberger to eventual game MVP Hines Ward (five catches for 123 yards and a touchdown to close out the game). Following the dramatic first-down conversion, Big Ben soon followed up with a one-yard run for a touchdown.

Still, fans were waiting for somebody to take charge and a play to open up some breathing room on the Seahawks and their quarterback, Matt Hasselbeck, who would pass for 273 yards in the losing effort. It came on what seemed, at first, to be a simple handoff and running play.

Roethlisberger took the snap, dropped back, and made that deliberate left-handed handoff as Willie Parker's arms opened high and low to receive the ball.

Ben Roethlisberger (7) took the snap, dropped back, and made a deliberate handoff as Willie Parker (39) opened his arms high and low to receive the ball. Parker broke to his right. Big Ben feigned a play-action fake as if still holding the ball in the crook of his left arm.

The Steelers running back moved toward the line of scrimmage, stopped on his right leg, and shifted slightly left, slicing through the hole provided by his O-line and pulling All-Pro guard Alan Faneca (66), hitting that space fast.

By then two Seattle defenders—one on his back, one watching Parker blast by—missed the potential tackle. Other Seahawks players were simply caught looking, blocked out of contention.

The Pittsburgh running back was upright and charging straight ahead by then, his right arm carrying the ball, his head looking downfield, striding past two more Seahawks defenders who seemed to

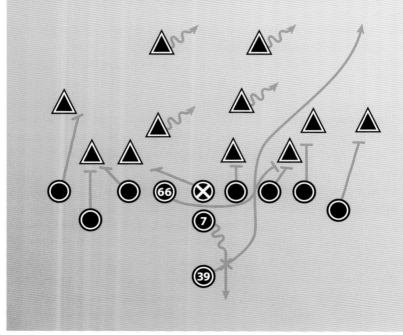

stagger at seeing the streaking Parker. Flowing into the open field, Fast Willie broke into a running stride.

He kept moving to his right, crossed the 50-yard line, looked left to check for any defenders who might need reckoning with, found no one threatening—unless you count the diving defensive back Etric Pruitt, and Marcus Trufant who jogged in depleted effort.

In the clear now, Parker ran into the history books, down the right sideline before his final move: an airborne leap headlong into the end zone.

Parker broke to his right. Big Ben feigned a play-action fake as if still holding the ball in the crook of his left arm.

The running back moved toward the line of scrimmage, stopped on his right leg, and began his shift slightly left, slicing through the hole provided by his offensive line and All-Pro guard Alan Faneca, hitting that space fast.

By then two Seattle defenders—one on his back, one watching Parker blast by—missed potential tackles. Other Seahawks players were simply caught looking, blocked out of contention.

The Pittsburgh running back was upright and charging straight ahead by then, his right arm carrying the ball, his head looking downfield, striding past two more 'Hawks defenders who seemed to stagger at the streaking No. 39.

Parker's acceleration on the run seemed to defy physical properties—everyone else seemed to be moving in slow motion. Flowing into the open, Fast Willie broke into a running stride most commonly noted with Olympic sprinters.

Footrace? You bet.

He kept moving to his right, crossed the 50-yard line, looked left to check for any defenders who might need reckoning with, found no one threatening (unless you count the diving defensive back Etric Pruitt and Marcus Trufant, who jogged in depleted effort), and ran into the history books, down the right sideline.

And if this wasn't enough—and let's note that NFL football is meant to be entertainment—Parker made his final move: an airborne leap headlong into the end zone.

The Steelers' running back would go on to post 93 yards for the day on 10 touches for 9.3 yards per carry—the third best in Super Bowl history largely because of the big touchdown run.

Bettis would add 43 more yards on 14 touches in his final game, his longest going for 12. Parker's Super Bowl record 75-yard scoring run turned the game Pittsburgh's way.

# Game Details

## Pittsburgh 21 • Seattle 10

**Location:** Ford Field, Detroit Michigan

**Attendance:** 68,206

**Box Score:**

| | | | | | |
|---|---|---|---|---|---|
| **Steelers** | O | 7 | 7 | 7 | **21** |
| **Seahawks** | 3 | 0 | 7 | 0 | **10** |

*Scoring:*
SEA Brown 47-yard FG
PIT Roethlisberger 1-yard run (Reed PAT)
PIT Parker 75-yard run (Reed PAT)
SEA Stevens 16-yard pass from Hasselbeck (Brown PAT)
PIT Ward 43-yard pass from Randle El (Reed PAT)

| Team | FD | RUSH | A-C-I | PASS |
|---|---|---|---|---|
| **Steelers** | 14 | 33/181 | 22-10-2 | 158 |
| **Seahawks** | 20 | 25/137 | 49-26-1 | 259 |

# WILLIE PARKER FACTS

Three professional football players have answered to the name Willie Parker. Willie Parker the Steelers' running back was an undrafted free agent in 2004, his first season with Pittsburgh.

The 5'10" and 209-pound running back played football for the University of North Carolina but with limited on-field appearances.

Parker has run a 4.23-second time for the 40-yard dash—the benchmark for speed.

In 2004, his rookie season, Parker played backup to running backs Jerome Bettis, Duce Staley, and Verron Haynes.

In 2005 Parker became a starter because of roster injuries (Bettis and Staley). His response? He ran for 1,202 yards on 255 carries for a 4.7 average per touch and four touchdowns. He also caught 18 passes for 218 yards (12.1 yards per reception) and a touchdown.

Pittsburgh's amazing playoff run and Super Bowl XL victory concluded that 2005 NFL season.

As a followup to that breakout year, Parker rushed for 1,494 yards during the 2006 campaign. He averaged 4.4 yards on 337 carries, and ran for 13 touchdowns. He also caught 31 passes for 222 yards (7.2 yards per reception) and three more touchdowns.

In 2007 Parker was leading the NFL in rushing with 1,316 yards when he was injured during the opening possession against the Rams in week 16 (broken right fibula). He ended up fourth. He finished with a 4.1 yards-per-carry average on 321 carries and two touchdowns. He also pulled in 23 catches for 164 yards (7.1 yard average per reception).

A two-time Pro Bowl pick (2006, 2007), Parker's presence on the field during the Steelers' 2007 NFL season wild-card playoff loss to the Jacksonville Jaguars might have yielded a different outcome. He retired in 2009.

# BLOUNT'S INTERCEPTION KILLS DRIVE

As Minnesota threatened in Super Bowl IX, Glen Edwards hit the Vikings' John Gilliam, the ball went airborne, and Mel Blount made the key pick

The Steelers had waited more than four decades to win their first championship. Just as the Steel Curtain had put this Super Bowl's first points on the board with a safety, they now needed to lock down the victory. Cornerback Mel Blount shared the responsibility.

A third-round NFL draft pick in 1970—and part of Chuck Noll's successful draft-oriented franchise rejuvenation—Blount played his college ball at Southern University, where he did double duty as cornerback and safety. Strong, smart, and super quick at 6'3" and 205 pounds, he would defend against opposing offenses for 14 years (1970–1983), all with Pittsburgh.

Blount's forceful intensity allowed him to blanket receivers with hard-hitting pass defense, an asset in this era of NFL football early in his career. As the rules changed to enhance the passing game and free up receivers, he adjusted and still dominated.

Mel Blount's forceful intensity allowed him to blanket receivers with hard-hitting pass defense early in his career, an asset in this era of NFL football. As the rules changed to enhance the passing game and free up receivers, Blount adjusted and still dominated.
*Getty Images*

His intelligence fit well with the rest of his fellow Steel Curtain defenders. Man-to-man coverage? No problem. Zone defense? Count on it.

His speed factored into many game-changing plays over his career, which included intercepting a pass in every season he defended his side of the line.

The Steelers cornerback who wore No. 47 even contributed some offensive punch, returning two interceptions for touchdowns and two fumbles for scores. Blount was so powerful and swift he returned 36 kickoffs early in his NFL career for 911 yards, a 25.3 return average.

You need that kind of defender on the field when you're trying to win your first Super Bowl.

Joe Greene, pumping his fist as he exited the tunnel from the locker room with the other Steelers running behind him, symbolized the relaxed intensity Pittsburgh would bring to this game. Power. Grace. Style. That's what this roster had.

Blount's interception—one of three on the day by Steelers Mike Wagner and Greene—played a crucial role in sealing the victory. Minnesota had pushed downfield and was in position to score.

Vikings quarterback Fran Tarkenton dropped back to pass as action commenced on and around the 30-yard line.

## MEL BLOUNT FACTS

| | |
|---|---|
| Total career interceptions | 57 |
| Total interception return yards | 736 |
| Total opponent fumble recoveries | 13 |
| Super Bowls (all wins) | 4 |
| Pro Bowl nominations | 5 |
| All-Pro selections | 4 |
| 1975 NFL interception leader | 11 |
| NFL Defensive MVP | 1975 |

An unblocked and gold-shoed L.C. Greenwood converged on No. 10, "Scramblin' Fran," who had dropped back so fast no other Steelers were near him. But Tarkenton wouldn't be running on this game-changing effort. His goal was to put the ball in receiver John Gilliam's hands.

Greenwood lifted both arms as the pigskin sailed past him near the line of scrimmage.

# Game Details

## Pittsburgh 16, Minnesota 6

**Location:** Tulane Stadium, New Orleans, Louisiana

**Attendance:** 80,997

**Box Score:**

| | | | | | |
|---|---|---|---|---|---|
| **Steelers** | 0 | 2 | 7 | 7 | **16** |
| **Vikings** | 0 | 0 | 0 | 6 | **6** |

*Scoring:*
PIT White safety on Tarkenton in end zone
PIT Harris 9-yard run (Gerela PAT)
MIN T. Brown recovered blocked punt in end zone (PAT failed)
PIT L. Brown 4-yard pass from Bradshaw (Gerela PAT)

MVP: Franco Harris

| Team | FD | RUSH | A-C-I | PASS |
|---|---|---|---|---|
| **Steelers** | 17 | 57/249 | 14-9-0 | 84 |
| **Vikings** | 9 | 21/17 | 26-11-3 | 102 |

> I just pitied those receivers as I watched them go up against Mel.
>
> **—Rocky Bleier**

# SUPER PICK

With less than two minutes before halftime of Super Bowl IX, the Minnesota Vikings had a first-and-10 at the Steelers's 25-yard line. Vikings quarterback Fran Tarkenton dropped back and looked for wide receiver John Gilliam (42) on the left side of the formation. He was wide open, but free safety Glen Edwards (27) streaked across the field and broke up the pass with an aggressive hit. Cornerback Mel Blount (47) caught the ball in the end zone for the interception and returned it 10 yards. The Steelers would go on to win 16–6, the first of four Super Bowl victories for the Steel Curtain dynasty.

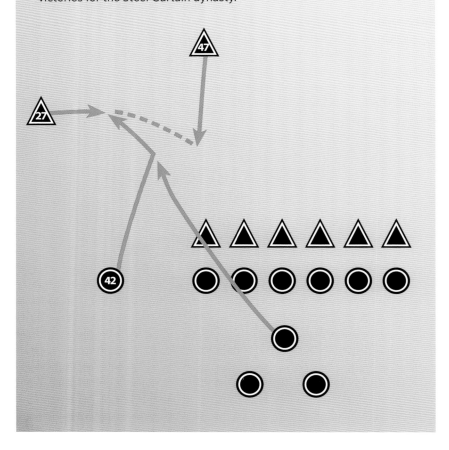

> Football's a physical game... and so one of the things I always wanted to do was to let people know this is my territory. If you come in here you're going to have to pay.
>
> **—Mel Blount speaking to NFL Films**

Steelers defensive back Glen Edwards, the 6′ and 185-pound playmaker, clearly anticipated the Tarkenton throw and cut toward the intended receiver.

As the ball reached the Vikings' wide-open and cutting Gilliam, who leaped up at the 5-yard line, briefly catching the toss with both hands, Edwards laid a hit on Tarkenton's intended target, his forearms planted directly above the receiver's upper chest, with the Steelers defender lifting both of his arms skyward as if he were lifting weights and throwing double uppercut punches at the same time.

Nasty hit. It did the job.

Gilliam's head snapped back, his body twisting on impact.

The ball went airborne.

Blount, waiting on the edge of the end zone, looked up almost as if catching a punt or kickoff and moved toward the arcing football as it reached its peak.

Gilliam, now sitting on the turf recovering from the hard hit, looked the other way as several Steelers anticipated the pick. Were he a cartoon character, stars would have been circling his purple helmet.

The interception settled into Blount's sure hands near the goal line as he ran downfield for 10 yards.

Such staunch defense helped win the game—the Steelers' first of six rings. Power running ensured it.

# STALLWORTH SETTLES THE SCORE

John Stallworth caught one for 73 yards in Super Bowl XIV to boost the Steelers to a 24–19 fourth-quarter lead and a win over the Los Angeles Rams

**S**uper Bowl XIV, the culmination of the 1979 regular NFL season, epitomized the peak of the Pittsburgh Steelers dynasty. Wins in Super Bowls IX (1974 season), X (1975 season), and XIII (1978 season) preceded it. The team now appeared before 103,985 fans at the Rose Bowl in Pasadena, California, and viewers all over the world. Pittsburgh was favored, but could it get the job done?

Some fans remember the uneasy feeling they had as the Los Angeles Rams led the game in every quarter of play. Upset in the making? It surely felt like it.

To start things off, the Steelers' baby-faced kicker Matt Bahr—a rookie and Penn State University product—claimed the first field-goal points with a 41-yard shot. Good kick, for sure, but for this sort of a game everyone wanted a touchdown.

John Stallworth's dramatic 73-yard pass reception for a touchdown put the Steelers ahead to stay in Super Bowl XIV. *Getty Images*

Lynn Swann and John Stallworth celebrate during Super Bowl XIV. *Getty Images*

Rams quarterback Vince Ferragamo watched Bahr's field goal from the sidelines. Once back on the field, Ferragamo—a name Steelers fans would hear way too often during the televised broadcast—played with poise and pass-efficient execution, going 15 for 25 on the day.

Eight different Rams players caught receptions. Even Lawrence McCutcheon, the Los Angeles running back, would complete a dramatic touchdown pass.

After the Bahr points, Ferragamo and his core of runners—Wendell Tyler, Cullen Bryant, and McCutcheon—took control of the game. Their first-quarter drive culminated in a one-yard Bryant touchdown run. Frank Corral, the former UCLA kicker, nailed the point after. This home-game Super Bowl momentum felt dangerous.

Los Angeles took its 7–3 lead into the second quarter.

The Steelers fought back the way fans expected they would. Franco Harris, who carried 20 times for 46 yards on the day—made one of those all-important one-yard touchdown runs. Bahr added another point.

# Game Details

## Pittsburgh 31, Los Angeles 19

**Location:** The Rose Bowl, Pasadena, California

**Attendance:** 103,985

**Box Score:**

| | | | | | |
|---|---|---|---|---|---|
| **Steelers** | 3 | 7 | 7 | 14 | **31** |
| **Rams** | 7 | 6 | 6 | 0 | **19** |

*Scoring:*
PIT Bahr 41-yard FG
LA Bryant 1-yard run (Corral PAT)
PIT Harris 1-yard run (Bahr PAT)
LA Corral 31-yard FG
LA Corral 45-yard FG
PIT Swann 47-yard pass from Bradshaw (Bahr PAT)
LA Smith 24-yard pass from McCutcheon (PAT failed)
PIT Stallworth 73-yard pass from Bradshaw (Bahr PAT)
PIT Harris 1-yard run (Bahr PAT)

MVP: Terry Bradshaw

| Team | FD | RUSH | A-C-I | PASS |
|---|---|---|---|---|
| **Steelers** | 19 | 37/84 | 21-14-3 | 309 |
| **Rams** | 16 | 29/107 | 26-16-1 | 194 |

# 1979: DYNASTY'S FINAL SEASON

In 1979 John Stallworth caught 70 passes for 1,183 yards (a 16.9 yard average per catch) and eight touchdowns. At the time, those 70 Stallworth receptions established a Pittsburgh franchise record.

During the 1984 season he'd pull in 80 catches (tied for second in the AFC that year) for an AFC-leading 1,395 yards (17.4 per catch) and 11 touchdowns. He'd retire after the 1987 season.

In 1979 wide receiver Lynn Swann, the other half of the dynamic Steelers pass-catching duo, pulled in 41 catches for 808 yards (19.7 yards per reception), and five touchdowns. He'd retire following the 1982 season.

Both men had entered the league with the Steelers back in 1974.

In 1979 Pittsburgh won the AFC Central division with a 12–4 record and .750 winning percentage.

In 1980 the Steelers would post a 9–7 win-loss season and finish third in their division.

An 8–8 record would follow in 1981.

Not to be outdone by Bahr, L.A. kicker Corral—a Pro Bowl player and All-Pro pick back in 1978, his rookie year—made field goals of 31 and 45 yards to boost his Rams to a 13–10 halftime lead.

This fourth Steelers ring would not come easily.

Many in Steelers Nation were waiting for the Lynn Swann and John Stallworth pass-receiving duo to leave their impression on the game. Of course that master plan was up to head coach Chuck Noll and quarterback Terry Bradshaw. The game after the break would determine everything.

Finally the third quarter arrived, and Pittsburgh fans got what they yearned to see. Bradshaw connected on a 47-yard pass to Swann for the first score of the second half. Bahr added one more. Okay, now maybe fans could go for that second plate of chicken wings.

But wait. Los Angeles had another move in mind—a trick play.

Catching the Steelers defense in an uncharacteristic moment, the Rams' running back McCutcheon hit Ron Smith on a halfback-option pass. The 24-yard pass reception, wide receiver Smith's only catch of the day, gave Los Angeles the lead. Again. Fortunately, they missed the point after.

Still, the Rams led 19–17 entering the fourth quarter. Not good—especially with the Steelers defense bowing to the Rams' offensive onslaught. Quarterback Ferragamo seemed to do whatever he wanted out there.

The Rams defenders had also punished Pittsburgh in other ways during the first three quarters: one series after his touchdown reception that put the Steelers ahead, an injured and dazed Swann had to leave the game following a leaping catch. Wide receiver Theo Bell, also sidelined, would be of no help boosting the passing game: the opposition had taken care of him on a punt return.

Fortunately Stallworth was still ready, willing, and able to turn this game into a win. But for great pass receivers to make game-winning plays, they need plans.

The plan was the play 60 Prevent, Slot, Hook, and Go. Even the name sounded like the medicine the Steelers needed.

After the third-and-eight snap, Stallworth ran the pass pattern. At 15 yards, he faked a hitch route, and the Rams defensive backs wavered and briefly faltered.

Protected in the pocket by his offensive line, Bradshaw countered, throwing deep in anticipation of his receiver's next move—a break toward the end zone.

After the ball left his quarterback's throwing hand, Stallworth cranked up his fluid pass route and accelerated past the Rams' pass coverage, executing the "Go" part of the play.

For a brief moment it seemed that the airborne football and the receiver would not converge, but Stallworth somehow, some way, caught the pass over his left shoulder on the fly near the 30-yard line—slightly off-balance but still fluid.

The 73-yard pass, catch, and touchdown put the Steelers ahead to stay. Bahr's point after made it 24–19, with Pittsburgh in the lead.

But Bradshaw and Stallworth weren't done.

After the third-and-eight snap, John Stallworth (82) ran the 60 Prevent, Slot, Hook, and Go pass pattern. He later related that it hadn't worked in practice during the week before the Super Bowl. This time it surely did. At 15 yards, Stallworth faked a hitch route, and the Rams defensive backs bought it.

Protected in the pocket by his O-line, Terry Bradshaw (12) countered, throwing deep in anticipation of his receiver's next move—a break toward the end zone.

After the ball left his quarterback's throwing hand, Stallworth cranked up his fluid pass route and accelerated past the Rams' pass coverage, executing the "Go" part of the play.

For a brief moment it seemed that airborne football and receiver would not converge, but Stallworth caught the pass over his left shoulder on the fly near the 30-yard line—slightly off-balance but still fluid. The 73-yard pass, catch, and touchdown put the Steelers ahead to stay.

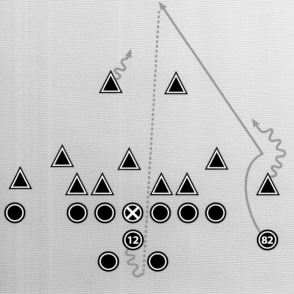

But Bradshaw and Stallworth weren't done. It had worked once, why not again?

For their encore presentation, on the next possession they'd connect on the same route (though a bit underthrown this time), and a 45-yard pass completion, again over Stallworth's left shoulder. This play set up the one-yard Harris touchdown run to clinch victory.

After leading 19–17 as the fourth quarter began, the Rams never scored again.

For their encore presentation, on the next possession they'd connect on the same route (though a bit underthrown this time) and a 45-yard pass completion, again over Stallworth's left shoulder. That play set up the one-yard Harris touchdown run to clinch victory. Bahr booted the final point.

After leading 19–17 as the fourth quarter began, the Rams never scored again.

Though Bradshaw rightly claimed his second Super Bowl MVP, and back-to-back awards, at that—14 completions on 21 pass attempts for 309 yards and two touchdowns (plus three interceptions)—Stallworth surely shared in the glory.

> During the course of the week we hadn't completed that pass. For whatever reason it hadn't worked in practice. I didn't hear the play [60 Prevent, Slot, Hook, and Go] and think, this is it, this is the one.... My initial read on the ball, my initial thoughts—and this is exactly what I thought—is that "Damn it, Bradshaw, you've overthrown me." And I really turned away from the ball and started to run.
>
> **—John Stallworth speaking to NFL Films**

# RANDLE EL HITS WARD

Wide receiver Antwaan Randle El's 43-yard pass completion to Hines Ward clinched the Super Bowl XL win

**S**uper Bowl XL MVP Hines Ward almost didn't play.

Two days before the big game at Detroit's Ford Field, the game that secured the Steelers' fifth ring, Ward badly sprained his left shoulder. Injured during Friday's practice on an innocent pass from quarterback Ben Roethlisberger, the hundred-percent-or-nothing Pittsburgh receiver had gone after a football thrown just a little too low.

A fierce competitor, even during his preparation for games, Ward had attempted to make the catch. The result: no movement in that shoulder. Not good for a pass receiver known for big plays, bonus downfield blocks, and game-changing catches.

Ward wore a sling on his left arm that weekend. A painkiller shot got him ready for the game that Sunday.

Even if you didn't know about the receiver's injury, Steelers fans looking on could tell something wasn't quite right. In the second

Pittsburgh wide receiver Antwaan Randle El, No. 82, throws to Hines Ward. This trick play locked up a Super Bowl XL Steelers win. *Photo David Drapkin/Getty Images*

quarter, Ward dropped an end-zone pass. Ward seemed preoccupied, unfocused, and tentative.

At the half, the Steelers were up 7–3—not a comfortable lead at all.

Things started to look better in the third quarter as Willie Parker's dramatic Super Bowl record 75-yard scoring run turned the game Pittsburgh's way, and the Steelers grabbed a 14–3 lead. They'd need an even bigger play to secure the win.

Roethlisberger moved up behind his center, took the snap, and smoothly spun right, the ball cradled in his upturned palms for the pitch to Parker, who had lined up directly behind him.

Parker received the ball, breaking left as the Pittsburgh offensive line blocked out Seattle defenders, some of whom still hadn't committed to the running back's immediate move.

Hines Ward, the intended receiver, was five yards off the line of scrimmage by now, slanting downfield even before Parker handed the ball off to Antwaan Randle El. Wideout Randle El, the one-time college quarterback, took the clean handoff from Parker on the reverse, already looking downfield for his man Ward.

Watch game film, and you'll see just 15 yards separating Randle El and Ward at this point, the two players evenly aligned on opposite sides of the line of scrimmage and ready to make the next dazzling move.

Pittsburgh Steelers wide receiver Hines Ward sails into the end zone for a touchdown on the pass from Antwaan Randle El. *Getty Images*

Randle El feigned a reverse run to the right as Ward began to high-step deeper into the Seattle secondary. Still, it looked like a simple reverse running play. Then the ball made its sure and steady way into Randle El's right passing hand, the way he'd done so many times as a quarterback at Indiana.

# Game Details

## Pittsburgh 21 • Seattle 10

**Location:** Ford Field, Detroit, Michigan

**Attendance:** 68,206

**Box Score:**

| | | | | | |
|---|---|---|---|---|---|
| **Steelers** | 0 | 7 | 7 | 7 | **21** |
| **Seahawks** | 3 | 0 | 7 | 0 | **10** |

*Scoring:*
SEA Brown 47-yard FG
PIT Roethlisberger 1-yard run (Reed PAT)
PIT Parker 75-yard run (Reed PAT)
SEA Stevens 16-yard pass from Hasselbeck (Brown PAT)
PIT Ward 43-yard pass from Randle El (Reed PAT)
MVP: Hines Ward

| Team | FD | RUSH | A-C-I | PASS |
|---|---|---|---|---|
| **Steelers** | 14 | 33/181 | 22-10-2 | 158 |
| **Seahawks** | 20 | 25/137 | 49-26-1 | 259 |

> It's like you chase something so long it becomes part of you.
>
> **—Bill Cowher**

# REVERSAL OF FORTUNE

Ben Roethlisberger (7) moved up behind his center, took the snap, and smoothly spun right, the football cradled in his upturned palms for the pitch to Willie Parker (39) who had lined up directly behind him. Parker received the ball breaking left as the Pittsburgh O-line blocked out Seattle defenders, some of whom still hadn't committed to the running back's immediate move.

Hines Ward (86), the play's intended receiver, was five yards off the line of scrimmage by now, slanting downfield even before Parker handed the ball off to Antwaan Randle El (82).

Wideout Randle El—the onetime college quarterback—took the clean handoff from Parker on the reverse, already looking downfield for his man Ward. Watch game film and you'll see just 15 yards separating

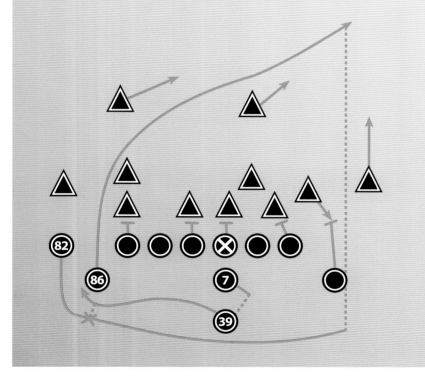

Randle El and Ward at this point, the two players evenly aligned on opposite sides of the line of scrimmage and ready to make the next dazzling move.

Randle El feigned a reverse run to the right as Ward began to high-step deeper into the Seattle secondary. Still, it looked like a simple reverse running play.

Then the ball made its sure and steady way into Randle El's right passing hand, the way he'd done so many times as a quarterback at Indiana.

Still on the move, he stopped, set, and threw the ball in one split-second motion toward his man Ward, who was now deep in the secondary moving to the right side of the field. Ward streaked toward the ball as it peaked in the air, looking up, running to catch the pass as a baseball center fielder does a fly ball deep in the gap. He got his bearings, adjusted, arms out, gloved hands open, and caught the long toss just five yards from the end zone.

Ball securely pulled in at the 5, Ward ran to the goal line, then long jumped and sailed for the score.

Still on the move, he stopped, set, and threw the ball in one split-second motion toward his man Ward, who was now deep in the secondary, moving to the right side of the field. It was a perfect spiral and exhilarating play in the making.

Ward streaked toward the ball as it peaked in the air, looking up, running to catch the pass as a baseball center fielder does a fly ball deep in the gap. Ward got his bearings and adjusted, arms out, gloved hands open, and caught the long toss just five yards from the end zone. With the ball securely pulled in at the 5, Ward ran to the goal line, then long-jumped and sailed for the score, the ball cradled in his right hand, the injured left shoulder and arm reaching out wide as he took wing into Super Bowl history.

Away from the action, Roethlisberger celebrated with his sure-bet offensive line that deserved as much credit for making it happen

"I've been waiting a long time to do this," head coach Bill Cowher said as he held the Vince Lombardi Trophy on the postgame podium. Brimming with emotion, Cowher placed the shining prize into the hands of Dan Rooney, Pittsburgh Steelers franchise chairman.
*Getty Images*

# WARD PASSES STALLWORTH

On December 20, 2007, against the St. Louis Rams, Hines Ward became the all-time Steelers receiving yardage leader. In the regular-season game, he had six catches for 59 yards, pushing the record to 8,737 yards, passing Pittsburgh wideout John Stallworth's record (8,723) in the process. Different eras. Both were standout receivers.

as the Big Ben–Parker–Randle El–Ward offensive 43-yard trick-play combination.

Jerome Bettis took it from there, pounding out short runs to kill the clock. By the end of it, Big Ben presented him with the game ball.

Super Bowl XL victory was secured.

"I've been waiting a long time to do this," head coach Bill Cowher said as he held the Vince Lombardi Trophy on the postgame podium. Brimming with emotion, he placed the shining prize into the hands of Dan Rooney, Pittsburgh Steelers franchise chairman, who had been there all those years.

It had taken a long time to get that fifth ring, and now Pittsburgh could celebrate.

# BRADSHAW DOMINATES DALLAS

Terry Bradshaw, Super Bowl XIII's MVP, connected with John Stallworth on a 28-yard lob for the first touchdown in a high-scoring affair

**T**erry Bradshaw had come a long way. When Bradshaw first joined the Steelers in 1970, a first-round draft pick out of Louisiana Tech University, head coach Chuck Noll had just begun to engineer his visionary plan for a dominant football franchise. The first phase of this draft-fueled effort reflected a hard-running offense and a tough, smart defense. By the time Super Bowl XIII arrived, Pittsburgh—with pass receivers John Stallworth and Lynn Swann emerging as vital links in the Black and Gold scoring machine—the passing game had also moved to the forefront. Bradshaw would now have to step up and take charge. Here in his ninth NFL season, he did just that.

Watching Bradshaw all those previous years, which had included two Super Bowl wins, Steelers fans saw their quarterback consent and comply with Noll's coaching influence and game plans and learn from that instruction—even

Pittsburgh Steelers quarterback Terry Bradshaw (No. 12) runs a play-action fake to running back Rocky Bleier (No. 20) during the Steelers' 35–31 victory over the Dallas Cowboys in Super Bowl XIII. *Getty Images*

if awkward sideline moments were witnessed: part lecture, part discussion. Growing pains.

Sometimes Noll glared with disappointment at his field leader, who called his own plays. Sometimes the maturing Bradshaw stared back. What fans really saw was a potent offense establishing itself: finally the two football personalities were thinking as one. Better yet, fans started

# Game Details

## Pittsburgh 35 • Dallas 31

**Location:** Orange Bowl, Miami, Florida

**Attendance:** 79,484

**Box Score:**

| | | | | | |
|---|---|---|---|---|---|
| **Steelers** | 7 | 14 | 0 | 14 | **35** |
| **Cowboys** | 7 | 7 | 3 | 14 | **31** |

*Scoring:*

PIT Stallworth 28-yard pass from Bradshaw (Gerela PAT)

DAL Hill 39-yard pass from Staubach (Septien PAT)

DAL Hegman 37-fumble recovery return (Septien PAT)

PIT Stallworth 75-yard pass from Bradshaw (Gerela PAT)

PIT Bleier 7-yard pass from Bradshaw (Gerela PAT)

DAL Septien 27-yard FG

PIT Harris 22-yard run (Gerela PAT)

PIT Swann 18-yard pass from Bradshaw (Gerela PAT)

DAL DuPree 7-yard pass from Staubach (Septien PAT)

DAL B. Johnson 4-yard pass from Staubach (Septien PAT)

MVP: Terry Bradshaw

| Team | FD | RUSH | A-C-I | PASS |
|---|---|---|---|---|
| **Steelers** | 19 | 24/66 | 30–17–1 | 291 |
| **Cowboys** | 20 | 32/154 | 30–17–1 | 176 |

> We won the Super Bowl. That's what we're supposed to do.
>
> **—Mel Blount**

to see that now-familiar Bradshaw smile on the field. That relaxed confidence came through in his play.

After leading Pittsburgh to a 14–2 record and a 1978 Central division win, Bradshaw and company were clearly the best team in football. But could they beat Dallas? The Cowboys had posted a 12–4 season to take the NFC's Eastern division title. Their roster was also stacked with talent.

Enter Super Bowl 13. Unlucky number? Not for the eventual winner.

The last time these two dominant 1970s teams had met in the big game—Super Bowl X—the Steelers had walked away with a win. Why not again? Problem is, Pittsburgh now faced the defending Super Bowl champs, a Cowboys team that had beaten the Denver Broncos 27–10 a little more than a year prior. Dallas coach Tom Landry would try to find a way to do it again.

Though some media types proclaimed the Cowboys to be America's team, an assertion the franchise promoted, the Pittsburgh Steelers fans and the players they followed disagreed. Trash talking prior to the game increased the rift.

Dallas linebacker Thomas "Hollywood" Henderson fanned the flames by offering publicized attacks on Bradshaw's on-field intelligence. In short, Henderson implied Pittsburgh's field leader wasn't all that smart: "Bradshaw's so dumb, he couldn't spell cat if you spotted him the C and the A."

If Henderson's intent was to intimidate, it backfired.

As if to answer to the charge, Bradshaw dropped back in his well-cushioned pocket, paused, and lofted a slight wobbling but sure-sailing pass toward the left side of the end zone. His receiver, Stallworth—double-covered or not—caught the football.

A 28-yard touchdown reception, sweet justice, and the big game's first points—it was the best play of the game because it literally silenced the questions. But Dallas would not go down easily.

By the first quarter's end, the score would sit tied at 7–7.

Dallas would go up 14–7 in the second quarter on linebacker Mike Hegman's 37-yard fumble recovery and return for a touchdown. Point after: good.

# BRADSHAW'S BOMB

Less than five minutes into Super Bowl XIII, Pittsburgh had a first-and-10 at the Cowboys's 28-yard line. Steelers quarterback Terry Bradshaw, who was derided before the game by Cowboys linebacker Thomas "Hollywood" Henderson, gave a subtle play-action fake to Franco Harris (32) and then dropped back to pass.

Steelers wide receiver John Stallworth (82), who had 115 yards on the day, streaked down the left side to the end zone. Three Cowboys defenders were around Stallworth, but Bradshaw (12) let fly anyway and perfectly placed the ball for the touchdown.

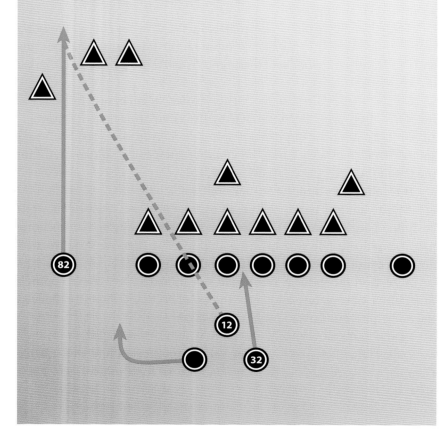

In comeback mode, Bradshaw again looked to Stallworth, who pulled in a pass and took the ball downfield 75 yards, legging it for the next score. Roy Gerela knocked in the next point, tying it up.

Bradshaw followed this scoring effort with a roll-right seven-yard touchdown pass to a leaping Rocky Bleier. A photo of Bleier's catch soon made the cover of *Sports Illustrated*, an issue of the magazine fans cherished. It felt good.

What an amazing first half of play. The score was Pittsburgh 21, Dallas 14 as halftime arrived.

As is sometimes the case, the third-quarter box score only reflected three points, a Dallas field goal.

The fourth quarter, now under a dark evening sky at Miami's Orange Bowl, proved to be another game in itself, with the Steelers dominating the first phase of it, and Cowboys quarterback Roger Staubach trying hard to pull out a comeback win at the wire.

Henderson made his second big mistake in the game's final quarter: he drove hard into Bradshaw after the whistle, still taunting the quarterback, but now with his on-field actions. A nearby Franco Harris stepped in and had words with the Dallas linebacker—uncommon for Harris. When play resumed, Harris's real retaliatory effort came as a 22-yard touchdown run through a hole in the line, right past Henderson and the rest of the Cowboys defenders.

On the next Steelers possession, Bradshaw threw his fourth touchdown pass of the day, an 18-yard shot to an airborne Lynn Swann.

Pittsburgh 35, Dallas 17. The lead looked sufficient, but not in a game like this.

To close the offensive show out, Staubach hit Billy Joe DuPree on a seven-yard touchdown pass with 2:27 still on the clock. Point after: good.

Next Butch Johnson stood in as the Dallas quarterback's target, catching a four-yard throw to bring the game to within five points. The Rafael Septien extra point closed the gap to four with 22 seconds left.

No matter. The Cowboys' onside kick proved as pointless as Henderson's trash-talking words about Bradshaw.

# STEELERS DIAL UP A LONG ONE

Lynn Swann, the MVP of Super Bowl X, pulled in his fourth and final catch of the day, this one for 64 yards and a touchdown

If the Dallas Cowboys had one fatal flaw in the 1970s, it was that some of their players talked too much before big games. Coach Landry should have issued muzzles in certain cases.

Not that the motivation hurt the Steelers.

Three years before Thomas "Hollywood" Henderson's comments about Terry Bradshaw's intellectual abilities as the two teams entered Super Bowl XIII, a different Cowboys player mouthed off before Super Bowl X. It was defensive back Cliff Harris.

"I'm not going to hurt anyone intentionally, but getting hit again while he's running a pass route must be in the back of Swann's mind," the Dallas safety Harris offered in veiled words of intimidation.

He referred, of course, to the lingering effects of a Swann concussion from the week prior against the Oakland Raiders in the AFC championship and how the injury might influence the play of

Pittsburgh Steelers wide receiver Lynn Swann (No. 88) makes one of his four catches—over Dallas Cowboys defensive back Mark Washington (No. 46)—in the Steelers' 21–17 Super Bowl X victory. Swann's fourth and final reception went for 64 yards and a touchdown. *Getty Images*

the Steelers wide receiver now. Swann had spent several nights in the hospital. Doctors had advised him that he could play, but another big hit might leave damaging consequences.

When Harris's words to the media reached the injured Pittsburgh receiver, Swann offered his own spin on the situation. He said, "I'm still not a hundred percent. I value my health, but I've had no dizzy spells. I read what Harris said. He was trying to intimidate me. He said I'd be afraid out there. He needn't worry. He doesn't know Lynn Swann. He can't scare me or the team."

Swann would surely take the field now.

Still, there was a little problem with timing and execution. In practice, Swann had trouble pulling in passes. The game proved to be another story entirely. He'd catch four passes in this Super Bowl—all of them memorable.

The first reception, a 32-yard Bradshaw toss down the right sideline, found Swann blanketed by defensive back Mark Washington. Still, the swift Pittsburgh receiver somehow found a way to dramatically pull the ball in and keep his feet in bounds. This catch was particularly meaningful, as it symbolized his successful return from injury.

"The most important thing to me when I stepped onto the field was to make the first catch," Swann later told NFL Films. "I had to make that catch."

That he did.

"Once I had that catch under my belt, I was back in the ballgame," Swann said.

The second pass saw the two Steelers players combine for a 53-yard completion. Bradshaw backed up to the goal line and threw a rainbow toward the 50-yard line and a moving Swann. It's the familiar highlight-reel reception you've seen many times over the years, easily a top-10 pick for Super Bowl history dramatics. Defying logic and the physical properties of gravity, Swann caught the ball while diving airborne and horizontal to the turf.

It's no surprise to Steelers fans he held on to the ball.

A review of game film over Swann's nine-year NFL career reveals other twisting, turning, striding, leaping, and lunging catches that

# Game Details

## Pittsburgh 21 • Dallas 17

**Location:** Orange Bowl, Miami, Florida

**Attendance:** 80,187

**Box Score:**

| | | | | | |
|---|---|---|---|---|---|
| **Steelers** | 7 | 0 | 0 | 14 | **21** |
| **Cowboys** | 7 | 3 | 0 | 7 | **17** |

*Scoring:*

DAL D. Pearson 29-yard pass from Staubach (Fritsch PAT)
PIT Grossman 7-yard pass from Bradshaw (Gerela PAT)
DAL Fritsch 36-yard FG
PIT Harrison blocked Hoopes's punt through end zone for
  safety
PIT Gerela 36-yard FG
PIT Gerela 18-yard FG
PIT Swann 64-yard pass from Bradshaw (Gerela kick failed)
DAL P. Howard 34-yard pass from Staubach (Fritsch PAT)
MVP: Lynn Swann

| Team | FD | RUSH | A-C-I | PASS |
|---|---|---|---|---|
| **Steelers** | 13 | 46/149 | 19-9-0 | 190 |
| **Cowboys** | 14 | 31/108 | 24-15-3 | 162 |

> In the end we needed him [Lynn Swann] to play that kind of game because the Cowboys were that good.
>
> **—Steelers safety Mike Wagner**

# SWANN'S SCORE

With 3:31 left in the game, Lynn Swann (88) practically sealed the Super Bowl X victory for the Steelers. Pittsburgh had a third-and-four on its own 36-yard line, and the Dallas Cowboys brought pressure—especially from defensive lineman Larry Cole.

Quarterback Terry Bradshaw (12) threw a bomb to Swann, who made the beautiful over-the-shoulder catch while on the run with cornerback Mark Washington (46) in close pursuit. The 64-yard touchdown was only part of Swann's impressive, four-catch, 161-yard performance. But that score gave Pittsburgh a 21–10 lead.

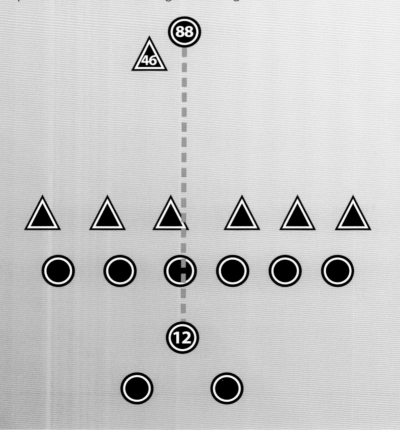

combine his hand-and-eye coordination and body-controlling precision. This reception was no exception.

That catch earned him style points, for sure. In practical terms, though, the field position he gained yielded no points. Roy Gerela would miss the field-goal attempt that soon followed Swann's amazing catch.

Confidence matters in big games. At times it was as if Bradshaw knew that if he got the ball in the vicinity of Swann—and far enough away from any defenders—that his receiver would find a way to pull it in. The third catch, a 12-yarder, added another to Swann's memorable day.

The fourth catch, the most meaningful in terms of establishing the lead and Super Bowl win, provided the crucial winning score. This catch came in the game's fourth quarter. With a little more than three minutes to go, third-and-four, the ball on the Pittsburgh 36-yard line, and Steelers leading 15–10, Swann lined up for the route.

The Cowboys' Washington, who'd had trouble with Swann all day, would fare no better this time. The Steelers receiver instinctively ran into the heart of the Dallas defense, into the middle of coverage, and took off.

After the snap, Bradshaw in the pocket, aware of the ongoing blitz, found enough leverage to muscle the pass deep. Two opposing results followed: Swann hauled in the long ball at the 5-yard line with the defender Washington reaching toward the Pittsburgh receiver a moment before he scored, and the Steelers quarterback was on the ground, unconscious from the Cowboys' pressure.

Helped from the field by safety Mike Wagner and running back Rocky Bleier, only later did Bradshaw hear the play's results: a 64-yard pass reception to Swann to put the Steelers up 21–10.

Swann and Bradshaw had saved their best for last. The Super Bowl X MVP, Swann's four pass receptions would total 161 yards on the day and the game-clinching touchdown.

As expected, Roger Staubach, with his customary effort—though he'd been sacked seven times during the game—made a bid right at the wire and posted a Dallas score on a 34-yard pass to Percy Howard with 1:48 to go. Staubach's game-closing efforts would falter and fail in the face of the Pittsburgh Steel Curtain.

# ROETHLISBERGER TACKLES HARPER

The Steelers quarterback made a game-saving defensive stop on Pittsburgh's playoff run to a Super Bowl XL victory

On that Indianapolis winter Sunday inside the climate-controlled RCA Dome, Steelers quarterback Ben Roethlisberger manufactured the improbable: a game-saving tackle on Colts defensive back Nick Harper, who was legging it to a fourth-quarter touchdown after recovering Jerome Bettis's goal-line fumble, another unlikely turn of events.

Classic Steelers football involves two basic fundamentals: running the ball on offense and stopping the run on defense. Big Ben's tackle was outside the playbook, for sure, but it was a major football play in Steelers history. Albeit unplanned and unlikely, the tackle was universally cheered by 'Burgh fans all over the world.

The Steelers held possession of the ball deep inside their red zone after a series of key defensive stops by linebacker Joey Porter and company. They were ready to put the game away for good: two yards to go for a touchdown, with four downs to do it in. Goal-line offense insists

Pittsburgh quarterback turned never-say-die defender Ben Roethlisberger trips up the Colts' Nick Harper, who had just recovered a Jerome Bettis fumble, and dashed downfield toward the Indy end zone. Without "the Tackle," as Steelers fans came to call it, no Super Bowl XL. *AP Images*

on plenty of power, so you wouldn't see speedy guys on the field for this one. It was a lock, right?

Not so fast.

Indianapolis Colts head coach Tony Dungy—a Steelers defensive back from his playing days, with a Super Bowl XIII ring himself, and a former Pittsburgh defensive backs coach and defensive coordinator under Chuck Noll—had held on to three potentially clock-stopping timeouts.

Three Colts timeouts weighed on the minds of those on the Pittsburgh sideline in that moment. As a result, Roethlisberger didn't take a knee three times in a row or run three quarterback sneaks (and possibly score), which were obvious options. Had he done the former, Dungy likely would have used those timeouts. Still, the Steelers could have put three more points on the board with a field goal on the fourth down. This, though, would leave Peyton Manning and the Colts offense, which had charged back dramatically in the fourth quarter, with some time left on the clock—time enough for a possible win or tie, even with no timeouts left.

Instead, Coach Bill Cowher and his staff, including offensive coordinator Ken Whisenhunt, sent Bettis off right guard on a Counter 38 Power play to hypothetically seal the win. It was a play the Bus had run many, many times before, but 5'11" and 235-pound linebacker Gary Brackett (smaller than Big Ben, mind you) had other ideas.

Brackett's Colts helmet hit the football, and all 'Burgh fans watched in shock as their hopes squirted from their man Bettis's sure hands—hands that hadn't fumbled once that season and never, ever had bobbled the ball at such an important moment in his career. The Bus hit a bump in the road and lost control. The brown ball popped backward. It seemed to happen in slow motion, with Bettis's head turning to look in the direction of the football as he fell from the hit.

The ball momentarily lay on the turf, up for grabs. After the initial play scramble of black and blue and white and gold, a furious scrum of desire and effort, Harper rushed in alone, picked it up, and began his mad dash downfield. Roethlisberger's immediate focus and football instincts drove him to drop back as a midfield defender. He turned following Harper. Harper moved to cut back in the other direction.

# Game Details

## Pittsburgh 21 • Indianapolis 18

**Location:** RCA Dome, Indianapolis, Indiana

**Attendance:** 57,449

**Box Score:**

| | | | | | |
|---|---|---|---|---|---|
| **Steelers** | 14 | 0 | 7 | 0 | **21** |
| **Colts** | 0 | 3 | 0 | 15 | **18** |

*Scoring:*
PIT Randle El 6-yard pass from Roethlisberger (Reed PAT)
PIT Miller 7-yard pass from Roethlisberger (Reed PAT)
IND Vanderjagt 20-yard FG
PIT Bettis 1-yard run (Reed PAT)
IND Clark 50-yard pass from Manning (Vanderjagt PAT)
IND James 3-yard run (Wayne pass from Manning for 2 points)

| Team | FD | RUSH | A-C-I | PASS |
|---|---|---|---|---|
| **Steelers** | 21 | 42/112 | 24-14-1 | 183 |
| **Colts** | 15 | 14/58 | 38-22-0 | 247 |

> That might be the biggest play ever in his [Roethlisberger's] career. My heart was going to my feet and back up.
>
> **—Larry Foote, Steelers linebacker**

# COUNTER 38 POWER

Jerome Bettis could run through any simple arm tackle, his legs churning and upper body powering through defenders. To stop the Bus, direct hits were required.

The play Counter 38 Power, simple in execution, capitalized on Bettis's strength. The play called for a short bowl-you-over run for yardage when the Steelers needed it—a first down or touchdown, you choose. He had successfully carried the ball on this play many times during his career.

In this AFC divisional playoff game, though, Colts linebacker Gary Brackett made that direct hit. Watch game film, and you'll see the Pittsburgh offensive line effectively blocking out defenders, opening up a hole, containing all except Brackett, who met Bettis in an RCA Dome standoff.

Brackett's helmet drilled that ball directly out of Bettis's sure hands, and this dramatic play followed.

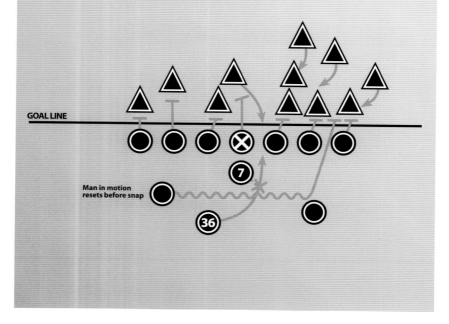

While Ben Roethlisberger's touchdown-saving tackle is his best remembered contribution in the playoff win over Indianapolis, Big Ben hurt the Colts with his arm, too, passing for 197 yards and two touchdowns. *AP Images*

Roethlisberger wheeled again and leaned toward the Colt with the ball—the ball he'd handed off to Bettis moments before.

Then, at the moment of truth, Big Ben managed to shoestring Indy's hopes of a Super Bowl run. A 6′5″ and 240-pound quarterback can make that sort of a play.

Harper, whose wife allegedly had stabbed him in his right knee the day before, carried three stitches right where Roethlisberger tackled him. The quarterback first handled the goal-bound Indianapolis defender with a stiff forearm swat, the way a grizzly bear handles its intended prey. Coincidence of circumstance or not, the Steelers' No.

7 slowed Harper down by the foot and amazingly downed the Colts cornerback as Pittsburgh tight end Jerame Tuman sealed the deal.

Wow. From Maine to Montana, in sports bars and in homes all around the city of Pittsburgh and beyond, unexpected cheering, then a sigh of deep relief, could be heard all across Steelers Nation. In the Pittsburgh Steelers' fabled history, this series of moments dished out a range of high emotion, low despair, then exalted release. But the action wasn't over just yet. A mild aftershock would follow Big Ben's extraordinary takedown.

The Steelers had failed to score and put the game away for good. The Colts now had the ball. To put it more specifically, Manning was in charge. It was Indy's ball at their 42-yard line with 1:01 on the clock—plenty of time for the Colts' take-charge quarterback to stage

## BIG BEN FOOTBALL FACTS

Born on March 2, 1982, in Findlay, Ohio, Ben Roethlisberger is the youngest starting NFL quarterback ever to win a Super Bowl (the Steelers 21–10 victory over the Seattle Seahawks on February 5, 2006).

Roethlisberger can also claim the following:
- Longest winning streak compiled to start an NFL quarterback's career: 15 games
- Highest quarterback rating by an NFL rookie (2004): 98.1
- Best completion percentage by an NFL rookie quarterback: 66.4 percent
- First quarterback to start two conference championship games in his first two NFL seasons (2004 and 2005)
- Named Associated Press NFL Offensive Rookie of the Year on January 5, 2005
- Victories in Super Bowls XL and XLIII, and an appearance in Super Bowl XLV

a comeback and squash all that Roethlisberger had just salvaged. This playoff game against Big Ben and his low-seeded team was simply a necessary step along the way, right?

But it was not to be. Indy reached the Steelers' 28, and then on consecutive second and third downs rookie Pittsburgh cornerback Bryant McFadden broke up passes to the Colts' Reggie Wayne, nearly intercepting the second one. Classic Steelers defense is all about stopping the pass, too.

The Colts were still alive, though, at least to tie.

That's when Mike Vanderjagt, the most accurate field-goal kicker in the NFL, swaggered onto the field. Another lock? Not in this particular game of twists and dramatic turns. Vanderjagt's uniform No. 13 proved unlucky this time. He booted the potentially game-tying 46-yarder wide right.

And that's how a number-six playoff seed Pittsburgh Steelers team dropped a number-one ranked roster of players heavily favored to win Super Bowl XL. In the end, the sixth-seeded, Black and Gold underdogs would win it all.

Finally Steelers Nation could celebrate.

As the game-saving tackle goes, Roethlisberger said, "I think I turned him enough times that he [Nick Harper] got close to me, and he couldn't decide which way to go, so now I just saw his leg and grabbed it, and luckily he went down."

Statistics show Big Ben went 14 for 24 and 197 yards in this memorable AFC divisional playoff game, plus two touchdowns and just one interception—along with steady composure along the way. In the end, it's the shoestring tackle that will be remembered when the numbers fade. That's the defining moment.

It was the XL factor the Steelers needed on the road to the franchise's fifth Super Bowl win.

# THE IMMACULATE RECEPTION

Franco Harris's amazing catch, run, and touchdown to beat the Oakland Raiders ranks as maybe the greatest play in NFL—not just Steelers—history

**T**wenty-two seconds remained on the clock. The Steelers now trailed the Raiders by a score of 7–6. Oakland had scored late in the game on a 30-yard run by their quarterback, Ken Stabler, to go ahead in this defensive struggle. Pittsburgh faced a sketchy fourth-and-10 on their own 40 and possessed no timeouts to slow matters.

Ever calm in a storm, head coach Chuck Noll called a 66 Circle Option pass play, one intended for wide receiver Barry Pearson, a rookie with zero statistical contributions that season, now appearing in his first NFL game. Not a good situation, but that's how many great plays are born.

Quarterback Terry Bradshaw, unable to find his intended receiver, somehow doggedly dodged the onslaught of the Raiders' silver and black jerseys and launched the ball off-balance toward Oakland's 35-yard line. A Hail Mary desperation pass, for sure.

Following the dramatic deflection, a second elapsed as the Steelers' No. 32 Franco Harris swept in and grabbed the gravity-bent and lazily wobbling pigskin before it hit the artificial turf. Terry Bradshaw's pass had bounced off Oakland defensive back Jack Tatum, though the Raiders argued the ball had hit John "Frenchy" Fuqua. *Getty Images*

The effort indeed looked like a prayer at best. Miraculously, that frantic petition was answered. Oakland safety Jack Tatum, also known as the "Assassin," and John "Frenchy" Fuqua met on a slam-bam collision course, with hard-nosed Tatum drilling Fuqua—who appeared stiff-legged as if he'd just been nailed by a sniper—to the Three Rivers Stadium artificial turf.

The football had other ideas at that point, as did Franco Harris, who had been blocking. He drifted downfield to provide another eligible receiver, a term which is maybe an understatement, considering what happened next.

A short second passed as the Steelers' No. 32 swept in and grabbed the gravity-bent and lazily wobbling pigskin before it hit the artificial turf. At that Harris ran—you might even call it a gallop, for all his fluid intensity—downfield for 42 more yards, just side-stepping and staying inside the goal marker to put Pittsburgh ahead 12–7.

Statistically it reads as a 60-yard pass from Bradshaw to Harris. NFL Films chose it as the greatest play of all time, and many Steelers fans who lived it—either the 50,350 who attended Three Rivers Stadium that Saturday or the countless fans who watched on television outside

## IMMACULATE RECEPTION PERCEPTIONS

Defensive back Jack Tatum—ever the Oakland Raider, one of the NFL's hardest hitters of all time, who later paralyzed the New England Patriots' wide receiver Darryl Stingley on a 1978 preseason hit—has insisted the football did not touch him on his collision with John "Frenchy" Fuqua.

Oakland linebacker Phil Villapiano—who defensively shadowed Franco Harris on the play and also accused Steelers tight end John McMakin of blocking him illegally just as he was about to tackle Harris after the reception—says that it bounced off Fuqua as well.

On the subject of the Immaculate Reception, Fuqua—also known as "the Count" during his playing days, with live goldfish swimming in his see-through platform heels—is slyly unforthcoming.

This play's drama once hinged on the disputed possibility it was illegal. In 1978 the NFL changed the rule that once disallowed two offensive players to touch the football consecutively on a pass attempt.

An inducted member of the NFL 1970s All-Decade Team, Harris's actions on the field have the final, famous last say.

Statistically the Immaculate Reception reads as a 60-yard touchdown pass from Bradshaw to Harris. NFL Films chose it as the greatest play of all time, and many Steelers fans won't beg to differ. *Getty Images*

the mandated blackout zone—won't beg to differ. Pop culture legend still debates who viewed the televised broadcast, and who couldn't—this detail is as controversial as the play.

Some did argue with the call, focusing squarely on the following points. If the football had ricocheted off fullback Fuqua and Harris touched the ball next, the reception, immaculate or not, would be ruled illegal. Two offensive players couldn't touch a pass in succession at the time, and that would nullify the Steelers' emotional win. The Raiders would have regained possession and won the game.

Then again, if the ball had deflected off Fuqua and then Tatum, the play was legal because the Raiders defender would have been the last to touch the football.

And finally, if Tatum alone had touched it, that too would have permitted Harris—named both United Press International's AFC and Associated Press's NFL Offensive Rookie of the Year that

# Game Details

## Pittsburgh 13 • Oakland 7

**Location:** Three Rivers Stadium, Pittsburgh, Pennsylvania

**Attendance:** 50,350

**Box Score:**

| Raiders | 0 | 0 | 0 | 7 | **7** |
|---------|---|---|---|---|-------|
| Steelers | 0 | 0 | 3 | 10 | **13** |

*Scoring:*
PIT Gerela 18-yard FG
PIT Gerela 29-yard FG
OAK Stabler 30-yard run (Blanda PAT)
PIT Harris 60-yard pass from Bradshaw (Gerela PAT)

| Team | FD | RUSH | A-C-I | PASS |
|------|-----|--------|---------|------|
| Raiders | 13 | 31/138 | 31–138 | 78 |
| Steelers | 13 | 36/108 | 36–108 | 144 |

> That was the play we had drawn up. Franco was the receiver all the way.
>
> **—Terry Bradshaw**

season—to legally scoop up the nearly incomplete pass (one that wasn't even intended for him).

Though two other NFL officials on the field withheld immediate confirmation of the touchdown, Adrian Burk, the back judge, indicated a score. No instant replay rule existed at the time, so the play could not be reviewed by video feed on the field.

NFL officials supervisor Art McNally, conveniently sitting in the Three Rivers Stadium press box, answered referee Fred Swearingen's questioning phone call from the field and confirmed that it was indeed a touchdown.

This turn of events was not without controversy either. Though the confirmation was made by McNally, and likely by using television

Fans display a "Franco's Italian Army" banner for Steelers running back Franco Harris during Pittsburgh's 13-7 victory over the Oakland Raiders in the 1972 AFC divisional playoff game on December 23, 1972. *Getty Images*

# THE IMMACULATE RECEPTION

Though it has been meticulously watched and broken down like the Zapruder film, the formation used by the Pittsburgh Steelers during the Immaculate Reception was pretty basic.

Facing a fourth-and-10 from their own 40, the Steelers had two targets flanked to the right and one on the left of the formation. They had a two-back set with Franco Harris (32) on the right. Harris was not a receiving option; he stayed in to block. But as the play broke down, quarterback Terry Bradshaw (12) eluded pressure, the pocket eroded, and Harris drifted toward the middle of the field.

There he became the lucky recipient of the football during one of the most famous plays in NFL history.

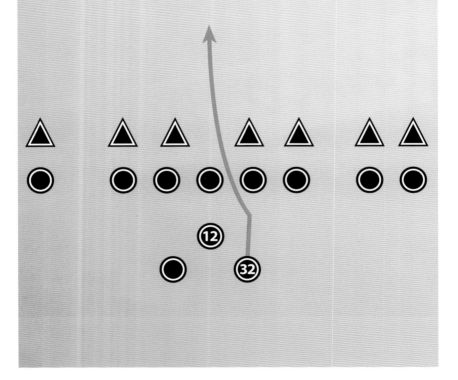

replay to validate the on-field decision (the first time ever in an NFL game and uncharted territory, though there's still that little debated matter of the televised blackout to cloud the issue), the NFL did not affirm it at the time.

The play is still shrouded in mystery, as no camera angles conclusively show what happened.

The Chief, Art Rooney, had left before the play to take the elevator to the locker room, where he intended to speak to the Steelers after they lost. He never saw the play live.

Many did. Pittsburgh Steelers fans are like no other NFL followers, and they rushed the field in exalted celebration. However, kicker Roy Gerela, who had scored all the Steelers points on two field goals prior to the touchdown, still had to attempt the point-after kick. Five seconds remained on the clock. A quarter of an hour later, he nailed the ball through the uprights.

During his WTAE post game show, Pittsburgh broadcaster Myron Cope described the play as the "Immaculate Reception," a phrase reportedly first conveyed to him by Steelers fan Sharon Levosky over the phone prior to Cope's on-air utterance. According to Levosky, her friend Michael Ord, also a season-ticket holder, first said it.

From a scientific viewpoint, the play stands—at least for one observer. Carnegie Mellon University physics professor John Fetkovich studied the NFL Films play clip in 2004. Based on the football's so-called momentum conservation and the way it moved through air space that December day, the professor concluded that the ball most likely bounced off the Oakland defender (who was running upfield) and not the Pittsburgh receiver (who moved down and across the Three Rivers Stadium artificial turf).

The play's magical aura carried the Steelers into the 1972 AFC championship the following week at Three Rivers Stadium. Though leading 10–7 in the third quarter, the Steelers would lose this game to the Miami Dolphins during the latter's undefeated run. Still, the Immaculate Reception foreshadowed things to come for the Steelers, namely four Super Bowls in seven seasons.

Such great things can happen in just 22 seconds.

# MENDENHALL FUMBLES A COMEBACK

Rashard Mendenhall drops the ball in Super Bowl XLV

**A**lready designated the visiting team in Super Bowl XLV, the Pittsburgh Steelers found Cowboys Stadium inhospitable as they faced the Green Bay Packers. Though Terrible Towels waved brightly all around—a testament to well-traveled fans, as always—it wasn't enough to turn momentum in their favor. Turnovers can mean the difference when teams are this closely matched, especially when one team has none. That was certainly the case in this game.

Ben Roethlisberger threw two interceptions into double-coverage, and one of them was returned 37 yards for a touchdown. These two mistakes didn't put the game out of reach, even though Green Bay turned them into points. When Big Ben connected with Hines Ward for a touchdown just before halftime, it surely felt like the Steelers had kept themselves in the game. The Packers led 21–10 at the half. But it wasn't over yet.

That is, until a big hit and fumble altered the course of NFL history.

Early in the second half, Rashard Mendenhall rushed eight yards for a touchdown. This felt like a turning point—momentum had shifted right out of the gate. It felt like old-school Steelers football. It looked like a memorable comeback was in the making. Kicker Shaun Suisham made the score 21–17.

But wait. Mendenhall had been plagued by fumble troubles as early as his rookie year in 2008. He had fumbled twice against Minnesota in Pittsburgh's third preseason game, overshadowing a solid running effort of 5.3 yards per carry and several memorable gains.

In an effort to curb an emerging trend, veteran teammate Hines Ward put a football in the running back's possession. A note nearby said, "Take Mendenhall's ball away and get $100 from him." Mendenhall carried that football everywhere with him. Rookie hazing of the old-school sort? No doubt. Unfortunately, it didn't work. Mendenhall fumbled again in

Packers linebacker Clay Matthews popped the ball loose from Steelers running back Rashard Mendenhall in the fourth quarter of Super Bowl XLV in 2011. The turnover led to a Green Bay touchdown drive. *AP Images*

the final preseason effort against Carolina. More coaching followed, but Steelers fans will always remember that inauspicious start, one that foreshadowed the events of Super Bowl XLV.

As the fourth quarter began, the Steelers had the ball on the Packers' 33-yard-line. The third Steelers turnover started out as a routine handoff from Roethlisberger to Mendenhall. Green Bay linebacker Clay Matthews intervened, hammering the Pittsburgh runner just as defensive lineman Ryan Pickett added to the one-two defensive punch.

Out popped the ball. Linebacker Desmond Bishop picked it up and returned it seven yards before getting tackled.

Heartbreaking.

What followed was a testament to Aaron Rodgers, as he quarterbacked the Green Bay offense to a 55-yard touchdown drive. The Steelers would follow with yet one more touchdown, but the fumble made the difference.

Though the Steelers won the time of possession battle by seven minutes and dominated the Packers in total yards (387 to 338), Green Bay had zero turnovers.

## QUICK NOTES: SUPER BOWL XLV

This was the first Super Bowl without cheerleaders, as neither the Steelers nor Packers employ any.

Ratings soared for this game, with an audience of 111 million viewers, making it the most-watched Super Bowl and broadcast in American television history.

Attempting to break the Super Bowl attendance record of 103,895 set at the Rose Bowl during Super Bowl XIV on January 20, 1980 (Steelers 31, Rams 19), an additional 15,000 temporary seats were installed in Cowboys Stadium. Actual attendance fell short by just 766 fans. Numerous delays involving the added seats caused some fans to be relocated, while others were offered refunds.

You could argue Big Ben's first-half interceptions put his team in the hole, but Pittsburgh crawled back in the game after those. Mendenhall's fumble gave the Packers the one big chance they needed to seal the win. They capitalized on the error. It essentially buried any hope of a comeback.

Super Bowl XLV MVP? Aaron Rodgers, of course.

While the Pittsburgh-area connection to Packers coach Mike McCarthy provided an interesting footnote—he was born and raised in the city, and grew up a Steelers fan—the loss was as tough as any.

# Game Details

## Pittsburgh 25 • Green Bay 31

**Location:** Cowboys Stadium, Arlington, Texas

**Attendance:** 103,219

**Box Score:**

| | | | | | |
|---|---|---|---|---|---|
| **Steelers** | 0 | 10 | 7 | 8 | **25** |
| **Packers** | 14 | 7 | 0 | 10 | **31** |

*Scoring:*
GB Nelson 29-yard pass from Rodgers (Crosby PAT)
GB Collins 37-yard interception return (Crosby PAT)
PIT Suisham 33-yard field goal
GB Jennings 21-yard pass from Rodgers (Crosby PAT)
PIT Ward 8-yard pass from Roethlisberger (Suisham PAT)
PIT Mendenhall 8-yard rush (Suisham PAT)
GB Jennings 8-yard pass from Rodgers (Crosby PAT)
PIT Wallace 25-yard pass from Roethlisberger (Randle El run)
GB Crosby 23-yard field goal

| Team | FD | RUSH | A-C-I | PASS |
|---|---|---|---|---|
| **Steelers** | 19 | 23/126 | 40-25-2 | 263 |
| **Packers** | 15 | 13/50 | 39-24-0 | 304 |

# ON THE OFFENSIVE

# MALONE'S RECORD TOUCHDOWN CATCH

Backup quarterback Mark Malone's unlikely 90-yard scoring grab was one of the few Steelers highlights of the 1981 season

**Y**es, that's right, a pass reception by Mark Malone, the Steelers quarterback, was a highlight. Sure, the Pittsburgh Steelers would disappoint fans this season and ultimately just break even with an 8–8 record. But this play stands in memory for both its symbolic and record-setting reasons. Yeah, in some ways it was just plain odd, but in the end it was fun to watch and effective in its simplicity.

Terry Bradshaw, the quarterback of the Steelers' dynasty teams, completed the pass on this play. In a way, it's ironic this record-setting reception would be thrown by Bradshaw to Malone, the all-around athlete and quarterback who would eventually take the reins from Bradshaw. For that reason alone, the event belongs in this book. First, let's look at some historical background to set the scene.

During his seven seasons with Pittsburgh, Mark Malone passed for 8,582 yards. Malone also shares the single-game record of five passing touchdowns with Terry Bradshaw and Ben Roethlisberger. *Getty Images*

The Steelers picked Malone, a three-year starting quarterback at Arizona State University, in the first round of the 1980 NFL draft. Pro scouts had the California-born prospect in mind for a number of player positions, including running back. The New York Jets had even suggested the latter idea during their recruitment efforts. After all, the guy was 6'4" and 223 pounds. He'd be a natural for many offensive roles, they thought.

In the end, though, Malone would remain comfortable in the quarterback position.

During his seven seasons with Pittsburgh, he'd pass for 8,582 yards and become the fourth-ranked quarterback in franchise history (he now ranks eighth on the list). He'd finish his career with both the San Diego Chargers (1988) and New York Jets (1989), retiring from football that season after just playing in one game. It should be noted that during his last time on the playing field, Malone's completion percentage locked in right at passing perfection (100.0), with two passes and two completions.

Not a bad way to go out, I guess.

## MALONE'S PASS RECEPTION RECORD

This Steelers record, as impressive as it was, was tied amazingly not just once but twice, once in each successive decade.

During the 1990 season quarterback Bubby Brister completed a 90-yard pass to Dwight Stone against the Denver Broncos, but not for a touchdown. Still, it tied the record.

Eleven years later quarterback Kordell Stewart tied the record after hitting Bobby Shaw to put six points on the board in a 2001 game versus the Baltimore Ravens. Then, in 2011, Ben Roethlisberger and Mike Wallace connected on a 95-yard pass play, setting the current team record.

Historically, for better or worse, Malone will always be remembered as the guy who was brought along in anticipation of replacing Bradshaw, who reigned from 1970 to 1983, a duty Malone later shared with David Woodley. But for one day, Malone, a quarterback, would become a pass receiver. He'd do it just one time. And that play would set a record.

Why Malone? He was a gifted athlete. As quarterback, he knew the receiver's pass patterns. Rumor had it he was also one of the fastest Steelers on the roster.

Pittsburgh had the football on its own 10-yard line—not the best position to be in if you want to score easy points, but great for setting up

# Game Details

## Seattle 24 • Pittsburgh 21

**Location:** Kingdome, Seattle, Washington

**Attendance:** 59,058

**Box Score:**

| | | | | | |
|---|---|---|---|---|---|
| **Steelers** | 7 | 14 | 0 | 0 | **21** |
| **Seahawks** | 3 | 7 | 0 | 14 | **24** |

PIT Harris 6-yard run (Trout PAT)
SEA Herrera 37-yard FG
PIT Malone 90-yard pass from Bradshaw (Trout PAT)
PIT Thorton 4-yard run (Trout PAT)
SEA Doornink 44-yard pass from Zorn (Herrera PAT)
SEA Brown 1-yard run (Herrera PAT)
SEA Brown 1-yard run (Herrera PAT)

| Team | FD | RUSH | A-C-I | PASS |
|---|---|---|---|---|
| **Steelers** | 17 | 38/162 | 22-13-2 | 205 |
| **Seahawks** | 19 | 33/96 | 25-18-0 | 260 |

the longest touchdown reception in Pittsburgh Steelers history. Not the full intention, but that was what happened.

On a simple hitch route to gain some possible breathing room, Bradshaw tossed the ball to Malone, who had broken into the clear. Malone had beaten the coverage to make it possible, and defenders perhaps saw him as an innocent decoy.

## MALONE'S FOOTBALL HIGHLIGHTS

Mark Malone was a 1980 Senior Bowl MVP. In 1981 the Steelers had tested Malone at the wide receiver position during a preseason game versus the New York Giants, a foreshadowing of the record-setting play to come.

In the 1984 AFC Championship Game against Dan Marino's Dolphins, Malone passed for a respectable 312 yards and three touchdowns in the Steelers' 45–28 loss. Unfortunately, the Steel Curtain defense of the Super Bowl years wasn't available for the game, and the Miami quarterback put up 421 yards and four touchdowns. Both offenses combined for an amazing 1,024 yards overall. What goes around comes around, as they say. Marino would soon be bested by another great quarterback: two weeks later in Super Bowl XIX, none other than MVP Joe Montana, who led the 49ers to a 38–16 victory over the 'Phins.

In addition to the pass play, reception, and run for a touchdown highlighted here, Malone passed for 10,175 NFL career yards that racked up 60 touchdowns. As a quarterback, he also rushed 159 times for 628 yards and 18 touchdowns.

Malone also shares the Steelers single-game record of five passing touchdowns (September 8, 1985, against the Indianapolis Colts), with Bradshaw (November 15, 1981, versus the Atlanta Falcons) and Ben Roethlisberger (November 5, 2007, against the Baltimore Ravens).

Malone caught the ball. Held it. Ran for daylight. He hustled the length of that Seahawks gauntlet and right into the Steelers history books.

The hitch route that set up Malone's record reception involves a receiver feigning a downfield pattern before stopping abruptly to catch a quick pass, in this case from Hall of Fame quarterback Bradshaw.

The idea was to catch defenders off guard, and this highlighted record play most certainly achieved that.

It was Malone's first and last regular-season catch and touchdown as a Pittsburgh Steelers receiver.

# ROETHLISBERGER SCRAMBLES FOR DAYLIGHT

Big Ben grinds out a dramatic 30-yard run to put the Steelers ahead, rallying from a down-in-the-trenches 15-point deficit

**Y**es, this is the same linebacker-sized quarterback who made the game-saving tackle against the Colts during the Steelers' amazing playoff run to Super Bowl XL. That he would produce a dramatic running play now against the Browns was also unlikely for several reasons. First off, Ben Roethlisberger had injured his hip the previous Monday night against the Ravens in Pittsburgh's victory over Baltimore. Make a long run for a touchdown? Yeah, right. Not even on the radar. Second, the Browns led 21–9 at the half. Any other quarterback might have folded and mentally mailed it in.

Would Mr. Come-from-Behind John Elway have given up back in his day? No way. Roethlisberger won't on this occasion, either.

Wearing that big No. 7 on his uniform like the now-retired Broncos playmaker might have provided some symbolic inspiration, as Big Ben and his offensive line held strong to fight back to within five points: Browns 21, Steelers 16. But the serious dramatics were about to come—you could almost feel it. Pittsburgh Steelers fans watching on television, and certainly at Heinz Field, no doubt thought: "I think we can win this game."

The Browns dominated the first half, at least that much is sure. Something positive must have happened in the Steelers locker room though, because the same defense that had given up 21 points now began to mess with quarterback Derek Anderson's momentum in the third quarter. Anderson had seemed confident and in control in the

Quarterback Ben Roethlisberger grinds out a dramatic 30-yard touchdown run to put the Steelers ahead, after rallying from a down-in-the-trenches 15-point deficit. By the end of the game, he'd have to stage one more comeback to win it. *Getty Images*

first two quarters but now faltered and flopped. The statistics show the Cleveland Browns offense managed only one first down and no points in the second half. Not good for them.

It was as if Roethlisberger now possessed that intangible energy Anderson had held prior to the break.

Pittsburgh had the ball and third-and-10 on the Browns' 30-yard line. As his receivers were blanketed by the Browns' coverage, Roethlisberger (6′5″ and 240 pounds) looked downfield, carefully surveying the options, until he made that decision all quarterbacks must make: time to run or just man up and take the loss.

But run he did. And the Steelers quarterback didn't do what some might have done. Forget about sliding once he got the first down. He just kept right on going. And going. Hines Ward laid into cornerback Leigh Bodden. Roethlisberger lumbered on past, then lunged airborne for a touchdown as the slight 5′10″ and 186-pound Browns defensive back Daven Holly provided no stop.

A pass to Ward for a two-point conversion and the Steelers went up 24–21. Terrible Towels spun furiously with circular exaltations.

But wait a second. Hold on. If the Steelers had any Achilles' heel during the first half of the 2007 NFL season, it might have been their kickoff and punt coverage—not linebacker James Harrison when he was part of it, but the unit as a whole.

While their multifaceted offense was powered by the pass-catching trio of Ward, Santonio Holmes, and Heath Miller to that point, as well as Willie Parker's running threat and Roethlisberger's return to early career form, by the end of this day Pittsburgh would drop to 27th in kickoff coverage (26.0 yards) and 23rd on punt returns (10.5 yards).

The problem wasn't with kicker Jeff Reed—his leg had done the job. As a scorer, he'd also gone 14–15 on field-goal tries to that point, his only "miss" on a 65-yard attempt in the "what if?" department. Likewise, punter Daniel Sepulveda had averaged 44 yards per boot, putting 17 of 38 punts inside the 20 on such opportunities. It was how those efforts had been covered.

As if aware of this flaw in the Black and Gold armor, the Browns' Joshua Cribbs casually muffed a kick that seemed briefly as elusive as a running rabbit, but then picked up the football at the goal line. Was

# Game Details

## Pittsburgh 31 • Cleveland 28

**Location:** Heinz Field, Pittsburgh, Pennsylvania

**Attendance:** 64,450

**Box Score:**

| | | | | | |
|---|---|---|---|---|---|
| **Browns** | 7 | 14 | 0 | 7 | **28** |
| **Steelers** | 3 | 6 | 7 | 15 | **31** |

*Scoring:*
CLE Winslow 4-yard pass from Anderson (Dawson PAT)
PIT Reed 28-yard FG
CLE Vickers 2-yard pass from Anderson (Dawson PAT)
PIT Reed 35-yard FG
CLE Edwards 16-yard pass from Anderson (Dawson PAT)
PIT Reed 30-yard FG
PIT Ward 12-yard pass from Roethlisberger (Reed PAT)
PIT Roethlisberger 30-yard run (Ward pass from Roethlisberger)
CLE Cribbs 100-yard kick return (Dawson PAT)
PIT Miller 2-yard pass from Roethlisberger (Reed PAT)

| Team | FD | RUSH | A-C-I | PASS |
|---|---|---|---|---|
| **Browns** | 13 | 18/40 | 35–16–0 | 123 |
| **Steelers** | 22 | 35/159 | 35–23–1 | 242 |

> I was ready to slide...but Hines [Ward] was downfield blocking, and when I get that close to the end zone, I'm trying to get it.
>
> **—Roethlisberger on his 30-yard run**

he fooling with the oncoming kicking unit? If the Steelers collectively drilled Cribbs then—several missed chances at him inside the 5-yard line—that thought would have been squelched. But no: that was of course when Cribbs slunk by, skirted the sideline, and ran to daylight himself.

# ROETHLISBERGER'S RUN

Quarterback Ben Roethlisberger completed 23 of 34 passes for 278 yards and two touchdowns, but he used his legs for the biggest play in the 2007 contest against the rival Cleveland Browns.

With Cleveland leading 21–16 in the fourth quarter, the Steelers faced a pivotal third-and-10 at the Browns's 30-yard line. Roethlisberger dropped back to pass, and the Browns's edge rushers looked ready to envelop him. Big Ben stepped up in the pocket, froze the defense with a pump fake, and then took off through the open hole in the middle of the line. The former high school receiver scrambled 30 yards for the touchdown.

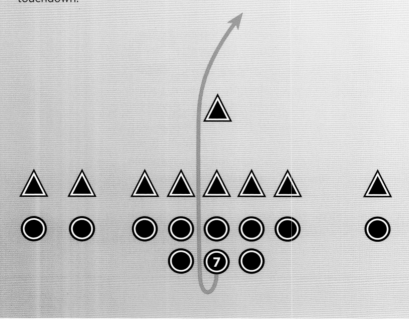

The Browns went up 28–24.

But Roethlisberger wasn't done just yet. His 30-yard touchdown run had set the tone for another comeback, almost as if this 100-yard Cribbs return was nothing but a bump in the road to victory, as if the Steelers' comeback win was now fated. Again, the hard-core fans had to be thinking: "I think we can win this game."

Big Ben, who now had the ball, definitely seemed to have the old-school feel of Elway's calm-in-a-storm confidence. It seemed scripted. In succession, Big Ben hit Holmes for 15. First down. Then Miller for another 20 yards. Then, with a third-and-nine facing him, Roethlisberger scrambled for 10 more. First down. Miller, an overshadowed workhorse for sure, caught the next ball from No. 7. One-handed at that.

Steelers 31, Browns 28.

Nothing now without that 30-yard run, though, nothing without that scramble.

The Browns had just one more chance, a field-goal try—granted, one for 52 yards and with just six seconds left. It was a satisfying miss. To imagine it otherwise was inconceivable.

Roethlisberger had thrown five passes for touchdowns less than a week before, which tied the Steelers record held by Terry Bradshaw and Mark Malone. Now his 30-yard run established one comeback and set the tone for yet another. The quarterback Steelers fans knew before his succession of bad luck following the Super Bowl XL win—his near-fatal motorcycle accident and his appendectomy, to name two major lowlights—had returned with a fury.

This 2007 divisional game marked the ninth consecutive time the Steelers had beaten the Browns. Big Ben was back.

Roethlisberger next made the 2007 AFC Pro Bowl roster with two other quarterbacks: the New England Patriots' Tom Brady and Indianapolis Colts' Peyton Manning. Following the Patriots' 17–14 loss to the New York Giants in Super Bowl XLII, Brady opted not to attend the Pro Bowl game. His replacement? The Browns' Derek Anderson.

# FOUR MEN AND A FLEA-FLICKER

Bradshaw to Bleier to Swann to Bradshaw to Cunningham: the Steelers' overtime flea-flicker that shocked the Browns into submission

Okay, you're sitting in a sports bar somewhere in western Pennsylvania. You're trying to kill a minute during the commercial television break. You turn to your buddy in his Hines Ward jersey and ask him, "Which receiver did Terry Bradshaw complete a flea-flicker pass to in the Steelers' overtime victory against the Browns back on September 24, 1978?"

Twenty bucks says he answers Lynn Swann or John Stallworth, and in that order. You tell him the receiver's name was Bennie Cunningham. His response: "No way."

Way. Bennie Lee Cunningham. The tight end who played all 10 of his NFL seasons with the Pittsburgh Steelers (1976–1985). The 6'5" and 254-pound Clemson University footballer taken in the first round of the 1976 NFL draft.

And when you're done telling your buddy that, he'll say, "You sure it wasn't Swann or Stallworth?"

The dramatic September 24, 1978, Steelers overtime flea-flicker and game winner over the Cleveland Browns included center Mike Webster and his O-line, quarterback Terry Bradshaw, running back Rocky Bleier, plus wide receiver Lynn Swann and tight end Bennie Lee Cunningham. Confused? So were the Browns. *Getty Images*

You're sure.

First off, consider the four quarters before the big play. Compared to the game during regulation, a slugfest of epic proportions, the overtime conclusion was pure poetry, with just a little bit of trick-play wizardry thrown in. Before that it was a lesson in guts that yielded glory.

Witnesses unfamiliar with NFL football could only hope to gain one conclusion from what was going on down on the field, something like, "Those guys seem to hate each other."

Want evidence of this from the hard-fought Three Rivers Stadium game? Try Pittsburgh's Steel Curtain dishing out plenty of hurt and then some, collecting four personal-foul calls during the skirmish.

# FLEA-FLICKER BASICS

As a fan, you know what it is when you see it, but often not until a split-second or so after you witness the flea-flicker begin. It's fun. It's full of fast, potentially fatal action.

By definition, the flea-flicker usually fakes a run to freeze or draw the defense. Its execution by the offense is the tricky part: a huge gain is possible, but a stifling loss of yardage or a costly turnover is also likely.

The quarterback usually takes the snap, either handing off or pitching the ball to a running back (Bradshaw to Bleier, in this case) or, in some instances, a receiver.

From there, the man with the ball sometimes runs parallel to or toward the line of scrimmage before making a lateral or handoff to another player (Bleier to Swann on this play). Sometimes that ball just goes directly back to the quarterback. Variations are many.

On this flea-flicker, Swann then got the ball back to Bradshaw, who found an open receiver downfield, namely Cunningham.

For the flea-flicker to work, the exchange of the ball must be fluid and flawless. Timing must be snappy. Academy Award nominations seem possible as players pretend intentions other than the actual trick play underway.

Fail, and the defense might read into the phoniness. The man with the ball might get tackled behind the line of scrimmage. The whole thing might crumble into foolishness—or worse.

One of the most famous (and somewhat gruesome) failed flea-flickers, this one on Monday Night Football, involved the Washington Redskins' Joe Theismann attempting this trick play only to have the unfazed New York Giants linebacker Lawrence Taylor tackle him, shattering the quarterback's leg, ending Theismann's career.

There could have probably been three times as many penalties. After one memorable reception, Swann took a full-on, shoulder-to-neck blow intended, or so it appeared, to not just stop but to maim. But No. 88 held on to the ball.

The Browns won the first half. The Steelers roared back in the second, amassing some 260 yards of offense to the Browns' meager 54.

# Game Details

## Pittsburgh 15 • Cleveland 9 (OT)

**Location:** Three Rivers Stadium, Pittsburgh, Pennsylvania

**Attendance:** 49,573

**Box Score:**

| | | | | | | |
|---|---|---|---|---|---|---|
| **Browns** | 0 | 6 | 3 | 0 | 0 | **9** |
| **Steelers** | 3 | 0 | 0 | 6 | 6 | **15** |

*Scoring:*
PIT Gerela 19-yard FG
CLE Cockcroft 43-yard FG
CLE Cockcroft 30-yard FG
CLE Cockcroft 41-yard FG
PIT Gerela 33-yard FG
PIT Gerela 36-yard FG
PIT Cunningham 37-yard pass from Bradshaw

| Team | FD | RUSH | A-C-I | PASS |
|---|---|---|---|---|
| **Browns** | 19 | 32/97 | 32-14-2 | 102 |
| **Steelers** | 18 | 37/139 | 32-14-2 | 200 |

# STEELERS IN THE PRO FOOTBALL HALL OF FAME

Several Steelers Hall of Fame players were part of this noteworthy flea-flicker against the Browns, including center Mike Webster, who snapped the ball. Here's the full list of inducted Pittsburgh footballers:

- Bert Bell: co-owner (1941–1946). Elected in 1963.
- Johnny "Blood" McNally: player (1934, 1937–1939) and coach (1937–1938). Elected in 1963.
- Arthur J. Rooney: founder, president, and chairman of the board (1933–1988). Elected in 1964.
- Bill Dudley: player (1942, 1945–1946). Elected in 1966.
- Walt Kiesling: player (1937–1938) and coach (1939–1944, 1949–1961). Elected in 1966.
- Bobby Layne: player (1958–1962). Elected in 1967.
- Ernie Stautner: player (1950–1963). Elected in 1969.
- John Henry Johnson: player (1960–1965). Elected in 1987.
- Joe Greene: player (1969–1981) and coach (1987–1991). Elected in 1987.
- Jack Ham: player (1971–1982). Elected in 1988.
- Mel Blount: player (1970–1983). Elected in 1989.
- Terry Bradshaw: player (1970–1983). Elected in 1989.
- Franco Harris: player (1972–1983). Elected in 1990.
- Jack Lambert: player (1974–1984). Elected in 1990.
- Chuck Noll: coach (1969–1991). Elected in 1993.
- Mike Webster: player (1974–1988). Elected in 1997.
- Daniel M. Rooney: president (1955–present). Elected in 2000.
- Lynn Swann: player (1974–1982). Elected in 2001.
- John Stallworth: player (1974–1987). Elected in 2002.
- Rod Woodson: player (1987–1996). Elected in 2009.
- Dermontti Dawson: player (1988-2000). Elected in 2012.
- Jack Butler: player (1951–1959). Elected in 2012.
- Jerome Bettis: player (1996–2005). Elected in 2015.

Pittsburgh had struck early, intercepting a Brian Sipe pass on the game's first play. This yielded a Steelers field goal. Cleveland kicked two more field goals in the second quarter and one in the third. It wasn't baseball, but the 9–3 score put the Black and Gold in the hole at the fourth quarter's start.

Two more Steelers field goals tied the thing with 2:35 to go. Time ran out with the game dead even: 9–9.

Overtime started off with a little controversy on a questionable fumble by Pittsburgh's Larry Anderson on the kickoff, which he'd fielded at the 11-yard line. After being tripped up by fellow rookie teammate Rick Moser, the ball slipped from Anderson's hands as he went down— down by contact, said the officials—and Pittsburgh retained possession.

After this, the Steelers proceeded to steadily drive to the Browns' 37-yard line. Second-and-nine. Run or pass? How about a little of both? Quarterback Bradshaw handed off to running back Rocky Bleier. Simple enough, but then Bleier handed off to wide receiver Swann for what looked like a reverse. That apparent reverse to Swann turned into a lateral back to Bradshaw.

And if the magic show wasn't confusing enough, Bradshaw lofted a long arching toss with his signature on it, and Cunningham caught it on the 3-yard line, then ran for the winning score.

It was also Bradshaw's 100th career touchdown pass. Amazing.

# JOHN HENRY JOHNSON'S 45-YARD TOUCHDOWN RUN

John Henry Johnson runs for a 45-yard touchdown to lead the Steelers to a 23–7 upset of their rivals, the Browns

**S**urely many of the 80,530 fans watching at Cleveland Municipal Stadium on that Saturday night in October hated John Henry Johnson's big power run and overall game performance. And that's the way it should be with franchise rivalries. Starting when the teams first met on October 7, 1950, this competitive matchup, often called the Turnpike Rivalry, has seen many a memorable game.

A member of the Steelers team playing against the Browns this night, the veteran Johnson was nearing the end of his career. His familiar uniform number, 35, matched his age. Though Johnson was a Steelers second-round draft pick in 1953, the 6′2″ and 210-pound fullback and halfback didn't choose to enter the league until 1954 with the San Francisco 49ers, after first playing one season with the Calgary Stampeders in Canada. With the 49ers, Johnson rushed for 681 yards (second in the league), averaging 5.3 yards per carry. In 1957 he was traded to Detroit. That year, he led the Lions in rushing (621 yards) and carried them all the

## THE STEELERS-BROWNS RIVALRY

The teams first met in 1950 at Pittsburgh's Forbes Field (Browns 30, Steelers 17).

Away games held at Cleveland Municipal Stadium between 1950 and 1995 were challenging for the Pittsburgh franchise, which posted a record of just 14 wins and 32 losses against the Browns at this location. Johnson's 200-yard game was easily one of the highlights during those years.

The Browns beat the Steelers 51–0 during the September 10, 1989, NFL season opener at Three Rivers Stadium.

On November 13, 1995, in a Three Rivers Stadium game against Cleveland, Pittsburgh won 20–3. Some fans wore orange armbands to honor the rivalry and the inevitable Browns relocation to Baltimore.

The two teams met for the final Cleveland Municipal Stadium game on November 26, 1995 (Steelers 20, Browns 17).

The Browns suspended operations after the 1995 season, concluding the original rivalry for a time, and the Ravens are officially listed as an expansion team, with a twist. The NFL deemed that team history would stay in Cleveland.

The Pittsburgh Steelers' Dan Rooney voted against the move, one of only two NFL owners who objected at the time.

During the 1999 season, after three years of suspended operations because of an NFL agreement, the Browns returned to Cleveland.

September 12, 1999, a decade after the 51–0 beating by the Browns, Pittsburgh returned the favor and pounded the newly established Cleveland team 43–0 during the inaugural 1999 season game (and first game ever) at Cleveland Browns Stadium.

way to the title game, where his Motor City team would beat the Browns 59–14.

Here, on this October evening in northeastern Ohio, Johnson was taking it to the Cleveland franchise again. Johnson would run for a Pittsburgh franchise record 200 yards this night and do it on 30 carries. In addition to his longest touchdown run of 45 yards—made with his characteristic and fluid style of moving the ball from one hand to the other as he eluded defenders—he'd score two more touchdowns from distances of 33 and five yards.

How tough were players back then? Johnson, like other NFLers, wore a single-bar face mask. Of course Steelers players like Bill Dudley

# Game Details

## Pittsburgh 23 • Cleveland 7

**Location:** Cleveland Municipal Stadium, Cleveland, Ohio

**Attendance:** 80,530

**Box Score:**

| | | | | | |
|---|---|---|---|---|---|
| **Steelers** | 10 | 6 | 7 | 0 | **23** |
| **Browns** | 0 | 7 | 0 | 0 | **7** |

*Scoring:*
PIT Clark 21-yard FG
PIT Johnson 33-yard run (Clark PAT)
PIT Johnson 45-yard run (PAT failed)
CLE Collins 18-yard pass from Ryan (Groza PAT)
PIT Johnson 5-yard run (Clark PAT)

| Team | FD | RUSH | A-C-I | PASS |
|---|---|---|---|---|
| **Steelers** | 28 | 64/354 | 11-9-0 | 123 |
| **Browns** | 14 | 12/96 | 29-13-0 | 121 |

in the 1940s wore no face protection at all. As Dudley and that historical era goes, you'll hear more later.

For many fans, the Cleveland Browns' Jim Brown was the star runner during Johnson's time, but on this occasion the Steelers defense would limit Mr. Brown to just 59 yards.

In the end, the Browns would earn a 10–3 record that 1964 season to lead the Eastern Conference, with one tie thrown in as well. The Steelers would have to settle for a losing record of 5–9 that year.

This same Cleveland team would eventually play the 12–2 Western Conference–leading Baltimore Colts (yes, Western) in the 1964 NFL

Pittsburgh Steelers Hall of Fame fullback John Henry Johnson carries the ball as Paul Krause attempts to tackle Johnson in the Steelers' 14–7 win over the Washington Redskins on December 6, 1964, at D.C. Stadium in Washington. *Getty Images*

# JOHN HENRY JOHNSON: A CAREER

Born on November 24, 1929, in Waterproof, Louisiana, he first participated in college football at St. Mary's until they dropped it from the program, then later at Arizona State.

He played Canadian football for the Calgary Stampeders (1953), and in the NFL with the San Francisco 49ers (1954–1956), Detroit Lions (1957–1959), and Pittsburgh Steelers (1960–1965). Johnson also ran the ball for the Houston Oilers in the American Football League (1966).

As NFL football history goes, Johnson was part of the 49ers' so-called Million Dollar Backfield that consisted of Y.A. Tittle, Hugh McElhenny, and Joe Perry, all of whom are in the Hall of Fame.

Johnson broke the 1,000-yard rushing mark in both 1962 and 1964 while playing for the Steelers. He was the first in franchise history to do that.

A Pro Bowl player, he played in the game four times (1955, 1963, 1964, and 1965), and three times as a member of the Pittsburgh Steelers.

And he was tough. How tough were players back then? Johnson, like other NFL players, wore a single-bar face mask.

On retiring, Johnson's career rushing yards totaled 6,803. At the time he was ranked fourth in the league behind Jim Brown, Jim Taylor, and Joe Perry.

As a pass receiver, Johnson caught 186 receptions for 1,478 yards. He also put up 330 points and 55 touchdowns during his time.

Johnson was inducted as a member of the Pro Football Hall of Fame class of 1987. Pittsburgh Steelers legend Art Rooney, who died the following year, presented him. Johnson passed away on June 3, 2011, at the age of 81.

Championship Game, which was also held at Cleveland Municipal Stadium. On December 27, 1964, just two months after Johnson ran all over them, the Browns shut out the Colts 27–0.

Considering Cleveland's great 1964 season, Johnson's 45-yard run, his overall running performance during this fall classic—and that of the underdog Steelers playing on the road and winning—is even more amazing.

# STEELERS SINGLE-GAME RUSHING RECORDS

During his first season with the Steelers, Johnson ran for 182 yards against the Philadelphia Eagles on December 11, 1960. He hit the 200-yard mark four seasons later in the October 10, 1964, Cleveland Browns game.

Six years would pass before John "Frenchy" Fuqua broke Johnson's rushing record on December 20, 1970, running for 218 yards against the Philadelphia Eagles.

In 2006 Willie Parker flirted with Fuqua's mark, hustling for 213 yards against the New Orleans Saints on November 12. Parker topped the record on December 7, 2006, in a game against the Browns, rushing for 223 yards. As a result, Parker became the first Steelers player to have two 200-yard games in a season.

It's interesting to note that these records were set twice against the Cleveland Browns by two different players and established twice by Johnson and Fuqua while playing the Philadelphia Eagles.

# BETTIS CATCHES STEWART SHOVEL PASS FOR SCORE

Kordell Stewart connects on a shovel pass to Jerome Bettis, who runs 17 untouched yards for the touchdown and an overtime win

**K**ordell Stewart was one of those gifted athletes who could do anything—literally. You'll find him listed as a Steelers quarterback between the years of 1995–2002 in most NFL histories. In truth, he also caught passes. He ran the ball. He punted. Rumor has it he waved a Terrible Towel in the stands when the Pittsburgh defense was on the field.

As a rookie in 1995, Stewart converted no fewer than 30 first downs: three as a passer, 13 as a receiver, and 14 as a rusher. Such diversity on the playing field had Pittsburgh Steelers broadcaster Myron Cope and head coach Bill Cowher driving

## THE 1997 STEELERS SEASON

Pittsburgh would go on to post an 11–5 record after this big win over Jacksonville. They'd secure their fourth consecutive AFC Central title. They'd earn their sixth straight playoff appearance. In 1997 Bettis would run for a career-high 1,665 yards on 375 carries, even though he sat out the last regular-season game as the Steelers had locked up a playoff position.

Head coach Bill Cowher would chalk up a personal achievement along with the team, as his six consecutive playoff appearances to start a head-coaching career tied Hall of Famer Paul Brown. Pittsburgh would fail to make the playoffs the following season.

Though the Steelers would beat the New England Patriots in the 1997 AFC divisional playoff, they would lose to the Denver Broncos in the AFC championship. This Broncos team went on to a Super Bowl XXXII victory over the Green Bay Packers, who had won it all the year before.

home the nickname "Slash" for the former University of Colorado quarterback. This designation attested to his broad abilities as a solid quarterback/wide receiver/scrambler and as a Steelers punter the following season (one boot, 35 yards). He'd later punt five times for the Baltimore Ravens in 2004 for a 35.4 average.

Stewart could scramble, for sure. He could make fingertip catches on the move. He could also rally for a come-from-behind win, as the Steelers had done three times that season.

The Jacksonville Jaguars always seemed to give Pittsburgh a good game. This one was no exception, and it required a big play for the Steelers to win it.

Here they were down again, 10–zip at halftime. No matter—Stewart was on the field.

It took some time, which happens when you're grinding out a 98-yard scoring push. Somehow, someway, the Black and Gold managed

Jerome Bettis played 13 NFL seasons (1993–2005), his last 10 with the Steelers, retiring after Pittsburgh's amazing playoff run and victory in Super Bowl XL. *Getty Images*

# Game Details

## Pittsburgh 23 • Jacksonville 17 (OT)

**Location:** Three Rivers Stadium, Pittsburgh, Pennsylvania

**Attendance:** 57,011

**Box Score:**

| | | | | | | |
|---|---|---|---|---|---|---|
| **Jaguars** | 0 | 10 | 0 | 7 | 0 | **17** |
| **Steelers** | 0 | 0 | 7 | 10 | 6 | **23** |

*Scoring:*
JAC Willie Jackson 8- yard pass from Brunell (Hollis PAT)
JAC Hollis 20-yard FG
PIT Hawkins 28-yard pass from Stewart (Johnson PAT)
    PIT Stewart 1-yard run (Johnson PAT)
JAC Mitchell 3- yard pass from Brunell (Hollis PAT)
PIT Johnson 19- yard FG
PIT Bettis 17-yard pass from Stewart

| Team | FD | RUSH | A-C-I | PASS |
|---|---|---|---|---|
| **Jaguars** | 16 | 23/73 | 31-15-1 | 194 |
| **Steelers** | 26 | 37/141 | 42-25-1 | 298 |

> I'm capable of doing a lot of things, but I'm a quarterback. I've said that, and I will always say that. That "Slash" thing, that's fine and dandy. But I'm Kordell Stewart, and I'm a quarterback.
>
> **—Kordell Stewart**

to go up 14–10 early in the fourth quarter, Pittsburgh's first lead of the game. Unfortunately this warm and fuzzy feeling wouldn't last long, as Jerome Bettis fumbled with 9:06 left. Hold the pepperoni pizza. Go find the antacid bottle. Jacksonville soon led 17–14.

But wait—the Steelers weren't done just yet in this seesaw affair. A 19-yard Norm Johnson field goal tied it with a little more than two minutes left. At the end of regulation they were still deadlocked. Would Bettis, here in his second season with Pittsburgh, redeem the Steelers in overtime? Would Stewart find a way to win?

For starters, Pittsburgh won the coin toss.

## "SHOVEL" PASS SENSE

Whether you call it a shuttle, shuffle, screen, or shovel pass— including intended and improvisational versions of the play—it generally works like this:

- The quarterback drops back as if to pass.
- The offensive line shifts into pass protection, holds that blocking set and effort for a moment, and releases the onrushing defensive line.
- The intended receiver lingers behind these rushing defenders, waiting on the ball.
- Outside receivers run clear-out patterns to open up room for the pass.
- If the trickery is executed correctly, the defensive backs will be led away with the deep-running receivers and the defensive line will have penetrated too far to stop a short toss.
- Lingering linebackers have to be dealt with once the intended receiver gets the ball.
- Fail, and a defender might intercept the short pass and make a big return with few offensive players to stop him.
- Succeed, and you might win a game in overtime.

> No one can exemplify this team's unselfish attitude more than Kordell Stewart. I'm sure he'll never forget some of the things he's had to go through, and I wouldn't wish them upon anyone, but he's buried the hatchet and handled himself like the consummate pro.
>
> **—Bill Cowher**

Next, with the ball in their possession, Stewart and company found a way to push downfield and into the red zone, where anything can and will happen if you watch enough NFL football.

There, on the 17-yard line, Stewart worked a little of his magic with a ready, willing, and able Bettis. Slash's sneaky shovel pass caught the Jaguars off guard, and the Steelers running back—his big hands firmly on the football this time—ran untouched into the end zone for the win. Stewart, a clutch quarterback on this occasion, went four-for-four during the game-claiming drive.

Inside that 439-total-yard statistic you'll find wide receiver Yancey Thigpen's 196 receiving yards and 11 receptions, a career high. You'll also note Stewart's 317 passing yards. Quarterback, indeed.

Fans also saw strong old-school Steelers defense when it counted. Jacksonville had tried for no fewer than 14 first-down attempts, converting only four along the way, thanks to the 1990s version of the Steel Curtain. The four-play, fourth-quarter goal-line stop sent the game into overtime.

# O'DONNELL'S TOUCHDOWN PASS TO THIGPEN

This second of two touchdown passes during the first half set the tone for a big 1994 AFC divisional playoff win

**S**teelers-Browns. Sox-Yankees. Celtics-Lakers (especially in the Larry Bird–Magic Johnson era). Rivalries make professional sports great. One game between the Pittsburgh Steelers and the Cleveland Browns was no exception. It was the first time the two teams had ever met in the postseason, though every regular-season game in their history seemed meaningful over the years.

The buildup for this playoff meeting started months before, on September 11, 1994, during week two of the regular season. In the Cleveland Municipal Stadium game, the Steelers won by the margin of a touchdown and extra point, 17–10. But the meeting was not without controversy. A Browns touchdown that would have tied the game at the wire was called back. That holding penalty proved costly to Cleveland.

Neil O'Donnell passes to a downfield receiver during the 1994 AFC divisional playoff game played on January 7, 1995. The Steelers won 29–9 over the Browns. *Getty Images*

**Dermontti Dawson (1988–2000):** As center, he got things started each offensive play—181 games over 13 seasons, in fact, playing his entire career with Pittsburgh. He was inducted into the Pro Football Hall of Fame in 2012.

**Neil O'Donnell (1991–1995):** As the team's third-round pick in the 1990 NFL draft, he quarterbacked for Pittsburgh for five seasons. Though he'll always be remembered as the guy who threw two interceptions to Dallas Cowboys cornerback Larry Brown in Super Bowl XXX, O'Donnell earned Pro Bowl selection in 1992 and made some big plays over the years.

**Yancey Thigpen (1992–1997):** In 1995 wideout Thigpen caught 85 passes for 1,307 yards and five touchdowns. A 1995 Pro Bowl player, he caught three passes for 19 yards in Super Bowl XXX. He made the Pro Bowl his final year with the Steelers as well (79 passes, 1,398 yards, seven touchdowns).

**Barry Foster (1990–1994):** In 1992, a Pro Bowl year for him, running back Foster broke Franco Harris's Steelers record for 100-yard games in a season: 12. This also tied Eric Dickerson's NFL record for 100-yard performances. That total helped Foster rack up 1,690 yards, a single-season record for the franchise. Though he also made the Pro Bowl in 1993, injuries dogged him for much of his playing career.

**Ernie Mills (1991–1996):** Wide receiver Mills hauled in a team-leading eight touchdown catches in 1995 and made some big plays during his career, including several in this highlighted game against the Browns.

**Eric Green (1990–1994):** Tight end and Pro Bowl player (1993, 1994), Green had 362 receptions, 4,390 receiving yards, and 36 touchdowns over his 10-season career, which also included time with the Miami Dolphins, Baltimore Ravens, and New York Jets after his Pittsburgh playing days.

**John L. Williams (1994–1995):** Fullback Williams came to the Steelers to finish out his career after playing for the Seattle Seahawks for years (1986–1993). A Pro Bowl selection (1990, 1991), this role player often added short but important yards.

**Tim McKyer (1994):** Defensive back McKyer played 12 NFL seasons for eight different teams, including Pittsburgh.

**Carnell Lake (1989–1998):** A five-time Pro Bowl player, including the 1994 season (his first nomination), safety Lake also made the NFL 1990s All-Decade Team, which is chosen by voters of the Pro Football Hall of Fame.

Later this season, the Browns traveled to Three Rivers Stadium on December 18 to decide the division winner. It was their opportunity for some payback, and you can bet that the disallowed touchdown in the season's first meeting was on the minds of the Cleveland players. The Steelers won again, matching their point total from week two. The 17–7 victory put Pittsburgh in the playoffs, and with a first-round bye.

The Steelers watched their televisions the following week as Cleveland entered the playoffs as a wild-card team, beating the New England Patriots in the first round by a score of 20–13, the Browns' Bill Belichick outwitting his old teacher, Bill Parcells, the Patriots' head coach at the time.

Next stop, Three Rivers Stadium—again. The January temperature was just below freezing during the midday game time, and occasional light snow greeted the Browns. The reception from many of the 58,185 fans in the stands, and the Pittsburgh players on the field, would be even chillier.

In the game's first quarter Neil O'Donnell crafted a long drive, taking command. Though it didn't culminate in a touchdown, Gary Anderson put a 39-yarder through the uprights.

In the second quarter the Steelers drove downfield again, this time for 47 yards and a score. Tight end Eric Green caught a two-yarder on that touchdown.

Not done just yet, Pittsburgh scored on its next possession: a 26-yard touchdown run by veteran John L. Williams through a hole provided courtesy of the Steelers' offensive line.

Along the way, the Black and Gold defense intimidated the Orange, Brown, and White. Vinnie Testaverde's receivers dropped passes, and his runners were flat-out stifled. You just knew this wouldn't last all day, and the Browns managed a field goal, a 22-yard shot by Matt Stover.

# Game Details

## Pittsburgh 29 • Cleveland 9

**Location:** Three Rivers Stadium, Pittsburgh, Pennsylvania

**Attendance:** 58,185

**Box Score:**

| | | | | | |
|---|---|---|---|---|---|
| **Browns** | 0 | 3 | 0 | 6 | **9** |
| **Steelers** | 3 | 21 | 3 | 2 | **29** |

*Scoring:*

PIT Anderson 39-yard FG
PIT Green 2-yard pass from O'Donnell (Anderson PAT)
PIT J. Williams 26-yard run (Anderson PAT)
CLE Stover 22-yard FG
PIT Thigpen 9-yard pass from O'Donnell (Anderson PAT)
PIT Anderson 40-yard FG
CLE McCardell 20-yard pass from Testaverde (PAT failed)
PIT Lake sacked Testaverde for a safety

| Team | FD | RUSH | A-C-I | PASS |
|---|---|---|---|---|
| **Browns** | 10 | 17/55 | 31-13-2 | 131 |
| **Steelers** | 23 | 51/238 | 23-16-0 | 186 |

After this score, the Steelers defense surely wanted to pick up where they left off. Having shut down the Cleveland running game, they now took aim at the passing attack. As evidence, defensive back Tim McKyer plucked a Testaverde pass and paved the way for another Steelers touchdown, returning the ball inside the red zone. O'Donnell was only too happy to oblige the favor and passed the pigskin nine yards to wide receiver Yancey Thigpen.

A 21-point second quarter makes a statement. The game was clinched by halftime.

Anderson provided the only score of the third quarter, a 40-yard field goal he made seem easy. It was also a time when some Steelers fans likely spent more time in the kitchen making sandwiches, with occasional glances toward the television set.

That is, until the Browns scored a touchdown in the fourth quarter. Even then Cleveland couldn't manage a two-point pass conversion, new to the NFL that season. And just to fine-tune the win, late in the game Steelers defensive back Carnell Lake sacked Testaverde in the end zone for a safety.

Pittsburgh's Barry Foster punched out 133 running yards.

The Steelers' Ernie Mills added 117 receiving yards.

Up 3–0 as the 'Burgh-Browns Turnpike Rivalry went that year, the Black and Gold would lose the 1994 AFC championship to the San Diego Chargers the following week.

MVP Steve Young and the San Francisco 49ers would then beat the Bolts in a Super Bowl XXIX blowout, 49–26.

# ZEREOUE'S SHORT RUN TIMES 2 EQUALS 12

Offensive points balanced a great defensive showing in the first-ever Heinz Field playoff game

**P**ittsburgh Steelers' division rivals include the Cleveland Browns, Cincinnati Bengals, and Baltimore Ravens. As Steelers fans can attest, bad blood often informs Steelers-Ravens meetings. Trash talk. Face-to-face staredowns. Especially when you're playing the defending Super Bowl champion in the postseason.

Though dressed for action and part of the pregame warm-ups, an injured Jerome Bettis still wasn't ready to take the field. A negative reaction to a painkilling groin injection that accidentally struck a nerve had sidelined "the Bus." Concern in Steelers Nation? Yes.

Amos Zereoue, his replacement, stepped in.

Pittsburgh surely needed Zereoue to have a big game. The Steelers had suffered a 13–10 loss at home to this same Ravens team back on November 4. Pittsburgh won 26–21 at Baltimore

Pittsburgh running back Amos Zereoue carries the football past former Steelers defensive back Rod Woodson for the first of his two touchdowns in the January 20, 2002, playoff game. *Getty Images*

in the most recent regular-season meeting on December 16. Evenly matched? Yes.

If the Black and Gold had any sort of foreshadowing edge in this playoff matchup, Pittsburgh offensive statistics reflected it. The Steelers had piled up 824 yards to the Ravens' 390 in these two regular-season meetings, despite splitting wins. Number crunchers gave Pittsburgh the edge. Matchup realists weren't so sure.

This game would determine more than statistics, though—it would decide participation in the AFC championship the following week.

# Game Details

## Pittsburgh 27 • Baltimore 10

**Location:** Heinz Field, Pittsburgh, Pennsylvania

**Attendance:** 63,976

**Box Score:**

| | | | | | |
|---|---|---|---|---|---|
| **Ravens** | 0 | 3 | 7 | 0 | **10** |
| **Steelers** | 10 | 10 | 0 | 7 | **27** |

*Scoring:*
PIT Brown 21-yard FG
PIT Zereoue 1-yard run (Brown PAT)
PIT Zereoue 1-yard run (Brown PAT)
PIT Brown 46-yard FG
BAL Stover 26-yard FG
BAL Je. Lewis 88-yard punt return (Stover PAT)
PIT Burress 32-yard pass from Stewart (Brown PAT)

| Team | FD | RUSH | A-C-I | PASS |
|---|---|---|---|---|
| **Ravens** | 7 | 11/22 | 37-18-3 | 128 |
| **Steelers** | 21 | 49/154 | 22-12-1 | 143 |

# AMOS ZEREOUE

Born on the Ivory Coast of West Africa, the 5'8" and 212-pound running back attended West Virginia University.

He played five of his seven NFL seasons with the Pittsburgh Steelers (1999–2003), coming to the franchise as their third pick in the 1999 NFL draft. Zereoue finished out his playing days with Oakland and New England.

His 2,137 career rushing yards came on 553 carries for a 3.9 average. His 137 receptions totaled 1,111 yards, averaging 8.1 yards per catch. He had 10 rushing touchdowns in 84 games, and two important scores in this one.

As with some other memorable matchups in Steelers history, strong offense established itself in the first half, and the defense did the rest, limiting the Ravens to 150 yards, seven first downs, and forcing four turnovers along the way.

Baltimore quarterback Elvis Grbac threw an interception on his first pass. Cornerback Chad Scott returned that pick 19 yards to the Ravens' 43, assisted by Steelers linebacker Joey Porter, who hit Grbac during his failed attempt. Pittsburgh safety Brent Alexander intercepted two more. Three additional errant passes were nearly picked off. Offensively, this was a straightforward in-your-face Steelers effort.

Pittsburgh kicker Kris Brown chipped in a 21-yarder for the game's first points. Zereoue ran for his first touchdown next, a one-yard effort. Brown added another point.

In the next quarter, Zereoue got his second score of the day, another one-yard Bettis-like ball carry, and Brown added one more.

Then, with Josh Miller holding, Brown kicked a 46-yard field goal to close out the Steelers' first half scoring. Brown celebrated as if he'd won the game. In some ways he had.

The score was Steelers 20, Ravens 3, as Baltimore's Matt Stover kicked a 26-yarder to close things down in the second quarter.

Amos Zereoue (center) celebrates with Kordell Stewart (left) and Jerame Tuman (right) after his first-quarter touchdown run against the Ravens. *AP Images*

The third quarter is always an interesting point in an NFL game. Some comebacks are staged there. Some momentum can shift. With 7:18 left in the third quarter, the Ravens' Jermaine Lewis offered change in the form of a punt return. It went for 88 yards, a postseason record.

At least Baltimore fans had something to keep them hanging on until the end.

That closure came swiftly on a 32-yard Plaxico Burress touchdown reception thrown by Kordell Stewart in the first minute of the fourth quarter. Burress (at an NBA-worthy 6′5″ height) simply outreached cornerback Chris McAlister (6′1″) on this one, as well as four other receptions during this game for a total of 84 yards. And yet these achievements lagged behind his December 16 performance against the Ravens (eight catches for 164 yards).

Stewart (12 of 22 for 154 yards) threw just one interception as the Steelers held possession of the ball for more than 40 minutes. In addition to Zereoue's solid game, Chris Fuamatu-Ma'afala, the Honolulu-born running back, offered support. The duo combined for 93 yards on 36 carries.

It took two guys to replace Bettis, but they managed it.

# FRANK LEWIS'S 76-YARD TOUCHDOWN CATCH

On the third play of a 1976 AFC divisional playoff game, Terry Bradshaw hit Frank Lewis for a long score in the 40–14 win over Baltimore.

**C**an you say offensive explosion? Frank Lewis was a 6'1" and 196-pound wide receiver out of Grambling State University picked in the first round of the 1971 NFL draft. In his 13 career seasons—the first seven with Pittsburgh, the last six with the Buffalo Bills—Lewis proved himself to be a passing target not named Swann or Stallworth.

Ironically, these two standout players, and their emergence as the most dominant receiving duo in the NFL, eventually contributed to Pittsburgh trading Lewis to Buffalo—not that Lewis wasn't good; it's just that Stallworth and Swann were great.

Pittsburgh Steelers quarterback Terry Bradshaw, No. 12, drops back to pass during the 1976 AFC divisional playoff game against the Baltimore Colts. Bradshaw was 14 of 18 for 264 passing yards in the 40–14 Steelers win. *Getty Images/George Gojkovich*

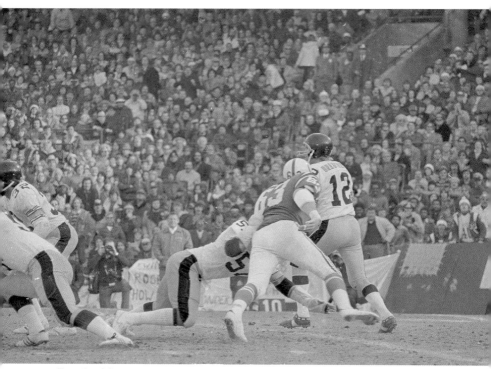

Terry Bradshaw was under heavy pressure from the Colts on the third play of the Steelers' December 19, 1976, playoff game, but he had already located an open receiver. An instant later Bradshaw unleashed a pass to Frank Lewis that turned into a 76-yard touchdown. *AP Images*

And that's why the Colts double covered Swann to set up the big play that followed. Bradshaw read this defensive move and adjusted. After all, he had another option at the time. So on the game's third play, the Steelers quarterback threw deep to Lewis for 76 yards, a touchdown, and the game's first score.

At times, it was that easy.

Bradshaw, the kind of team leader who could alternately drive you nuts with knuckleheaded turnovers and make you roar with approval on pass plays like this, had clearly slept well the night before. He was on. The Colts were in trouble. The big play had made a statement.

Roy Gerela, who also had that ability to thrill and test a fan's patience, missed the point-after attempt following the Bradshaw-to-Lewis dramatics. Not to worry about his leg just yet—he kicked a 45-yard field goal for the next score.

Baltimore scored next—a 17-yard pass for a touchdown, and added the point after—but Reggie Harrison, who had blocked the big punt in Super Bowl X, ran for a yard and the touchdown. Gerela made this one.

# Game Details

## Pittsburgh 40 • Baltimore 14

**Location:** Memorial Stadium, Baltimore, Maryland

**Attendance:** 60,020

**Box Score:**

| | | | | | |
|---|---|---|---|---|---|
| **Steelers** | 9 | 17 | 0 | 14 | **40** |
| **Colts** | 7 | 0 | 0 | 7 | **14** |

*Scoring:*
PIT Lewis 76-yard pass from Bradshaw (Gerela PAT failed)
PIT Gerela 45-yard FG
BAL Carr 17-yard pass from Jones (Linhart PAT)
PIT Harrison 1-yard run (Gerela PAT)
PIT Swann 29-yard pass from Bradshaw (Gerela PAT)
PIT Gerela 25-yard FG
PIT Swann 11-yard pass from Bradshaw (Gerela PAT)
BAL Leaks 1-yard run (Linhart PAT)
PIT Harrison 10-yard run (Mansfield PAT)

| Team | FD | RUSH | A-C-I | PASS |
|---|---|---|---|---|
| **Steelers** | 29 | 40/225 | 24-19-0 | 301 |
| **Colts** | 16 | 23/71 | 25-11-2 | 99 |

Next Swann got open for a 29-yard pass from Bradshaw, scoring on the play. Gerela knocked in the point after.

Done? Hardly. Gerela hit a 25-yard field goal to finish out the half: Steelers 26, Colts 7.

Whatever happened in the halftime locker rooms inspired the defenses to shut both offenses down, as no one scored during the game's third quarter.

Both teams woke up from their sleepwalking in the fourth quarter—the score still sitting at 26–7, where they left it before halftime—and decided to put some more scores on the board. Swann pulled in an 11-yard Bradshaw throw for a touchdown, and Gerela chipped in another point.

Baltimore's Roosevelt Leaks legged one yard for the first Colts score since the initial quarter, and the point after was good. But the game was still out of reach, Colts fans.

# WHAT ABOUT GERELA?

Roy Gerela's kicking career spanned 11 seasons, eight of them with the Steelers (1971–1978).

Canadian born, he attended New Mexico State University. Houston took him in the fourth round of the 1969 AFL-NFL draft. He played two seasons with the Oilers (1969, 1970).

During his career, he made 184 of 306 field-goal attempts (60.1 percent), his longest stretching to 50 yards (during his first year with the AFL Oilers). Gerela aced 351 of 365 extra point tries (96.2 percent). Total points in one AFL and 10 NFL seasons: 903.

He punted frequently during his first year in professional football (AFL): 41 boots for 1,656 yards and a 40.4 average, his longest going 70. Ironically he punted only once in the NFL, in 1972, and for 29 yards.

He won three Super Bowl rings during his time with Pittsburgh.

In the 1970s, select Three Rivers Stadium fans named themselves "Gerela's Gorillas" in his honor.

And just for good measure, because he's dominating this part of the book, Harrison scampered for 10 yards and a touchdown. The point after put the Steelers up by 26.

Wideout Lewis's receiving yards on the day totaled 103. Franco Harris rushed for 132 of the 526 total Steelers offensive package this game.

After he was traded from the Pittsburgh Steelers, Lewis flourished with the Buffalo Bills, even making the Pro Bowl team during the 1981 season, when he grabbed 70 passes for 1,244 yards (17.8 yards per catch) and four touchdowns, his longest reception going for 33 yards that regular season.

No stranger to the long pass reception, he scored a touchdown on a 92-yarder in 1978 (thrown by quarterback Joe Ferguson), his first year with the Bills—a career mark for both players. In his first game wearing the Buffalo colors, he stung Pittsburgh with a 22-yard touchdown reception. "Remember me, guys?"

By the end of his career, Lewis pulled in 397 receptions for 6,724 yards (16.9 average per catch), and 40 touchdowns. He also gained 146 yards on 12 carries for a 12.2 average and a touchdown.

In a bizarre postscript to the game, after play had ended, a single-engine plane crashed into the upper deck of Baltimore's Memorial Stadium. Many fans had exited prior to the incident, and no one was injured. Officials arrested the pilot in violation of safety laws. No word was given as to whether he was a Colts or Steelers fan.

# MR. VERSATILE, BILL DUDLEY

Bill Dudley's up-the-middle trap play in his first NFL game started a memorable career

**V**ersatile as a Swiss Army knife, Bill Dudley rushed for yardage, ran back kickoffs, returned punts, and more. He was the most notable Steelers player in the franchise's first two decades, and he played tailback for Pittsburgh in 1942, 1945, and 1946.

Just 5'10" and 182 pounds, the University of Virginia tailback and the school's first All-American, he was taken by the Steelers in the first round of the 1942 draft. William McGarvey "Bullet Bill" Dudley, also known as the "the Bluefield Bullet" to honor his town of birth, signed his first $5,000 contract to cover expenses. "There was a war coming on, and I wanted to get a little bit of money until I went into the service," Dudley has said.

Though Dudley became an official member of the Army Air Corps in September of his rookie season, he didn't see military service until after the 11 scheduled games played out. He made his mark in football from the start, almost as if he didn't have any time to waste.

Hall of Fame player Bill Dudley carries the football for the Pittsburgh Steelers in a September 29, 1946, game against the Washington Redskins that went into the record books as a 14–14 tie. *Getty Images*

During the 1942 season opener against the Philadelphia Eagles, for instance, his first NFL and Steelers game ever, Dudley ran 44 yards for a touchdown on an up-the-middle trap play for Pittsburgh's first score. That effort, drive, and will to succeed would inform his career, and this play exemplifies his talent. Though Dudley would run for 107 yards on the day, the Steelers would lose this game but eventually post a winning 7–4 record on the season—their best in franchise history.

Dudley could boast well-rounded statistics from his rookie season. His 696 rushing yards on 162 touches for a 4.3 average and five touchdowns led the NFL and the Steelers. He returned 11 kickoffs for 298 yards and an average of 27.1 for each run back—one even went for a touchdown. In addition, he returned 20 punts for 271 yards and a 13.6 average. Dudley also snagged three interceptions for a 20-yard return average totaling 60 and passed for 438 yards (35 attempts for 94 completions and a 37.2 completion percentage). His six touchdowns in

1942 led the team, and he even caught one pass for 24 yards. He played most of the 60 available minutes each game.

During his wartime absence, and a time of NFL player shortages, the Phil-Pitt Eagles or Steagles (1943), and the Card-Pitts (1944) were created. The former team involved morphing rosters with the Philadelphia Eagles. The latter group reflected a merge with the

---

# Game Details

## Eagles 24 • Steelers 14

**Location:** Forbes Field, Pittsburgh, Pennsylvania

**Attendance:** 13,349

**Box Score:**

| | | | | | |
|---|---|---|---|---|---|
| **Eagles** | 7 | 7 | 3 | 7 | **24** |
| **Steelers** | 7 | 0 | 0 | 7 | **14** |

*Scoring:*
PIT Dudley 44-yard run (Binotto PAT)
PHI Davis 3-yard run (Barnum PAT)
PHI Supulski 41-yard pass from Thompson (Graves PAT)
PHI Barnum 24-yard FG
PHI Meyer 12-yard pass from Thompson (Barnum PAT)
PIT Looney 24-yard pass from Dudley (Riffle PAT)

> We had a lot of fun. Pittsburgh in 1942 was probably one of the most fun years I ever had. I didn't know anything about Pittsburgh. . . . All the steel mills were in full blast. You couldn't see the sun for the smoke.
>
> **—Bill Dudley**

## WHIZZER WHITE: THE OTHER STEELERS RUSHING LEADER

On September 20, 1933, Art Rooney's franchise, then playing under the name of Pittsburgh Pirates, lost its first football game ever, 23–2, to the New York Giants.

Throughout the Depression-era 1930s, the organization would finish no higher than a divisional second place. One highlight from this first decade of Steelers history involved the 1938 signing of Byron "Whizzer" White—halfback, tailback, and future U.S. Supreme Court Justice. And, for the record, sources indicate the nickname annoyed him.

His $15,800 contract made him the highest-paid NFL player, but he would only be on the Pittsburgh roster one season (1938), a time in which he led the NFL in rushing with 567 yards on 152 carries. Two years later with the Lions in 1940 (yes, White and Dudley both went there after their Pittsburgh playing days), White also rushed for a league-leading 514 yards on 146 touches.

White played one more NFL season before serving his country with the U.S. Navy during World War II. After returning home he attended law school and then spent 31 years as a U.S. Supreme Court Justice, retiring in 1993.

White and Dudley both led the league in rushing twice.

Chicago Cardinals, yielding the Card-Pitts tag. The two-year team record during this phase of franchise history: 5–14–1. The Card-Pitts team did set one long-standing franchise record though: the only winless season (0–10).

After returning from World War II, Dudley played just four 1945 games, then in 1946 he led the team and NFL in rushing again (604 yards). By 1947 he was gone to Detroit, though the Steelers finished 8–4, tied for the Eastern Division that season. They faced the Eagles

# TRAP-PLAY TRICKERY

It's likely an ongoing trap play if you see an opening expand at the line of scrimmage as linemen block and trap defenders to make a gap for the running back to hustle through.

A defender is sometimes double-teamed and/or a playside linebacker is blocked as the play unfolds, instantly suggesting where the ball and runner will go. Should the linebacker read the play, he can step right into the area where the hole will be created and shut the running back down.

Often the running back will shadow his double-teaming linemen to read which side the hole might develop on, and he'll slip on through to daylight—left, right, rolling toward yardage.

Once into the secondary, if the blocking proves successful, a long run such as Bill Dudley's 44-yard opening day September 1942 touchdown—a trap play that developed out of the single-wing formation—might occur.

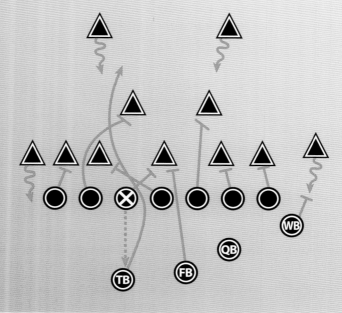

Used by the Steelers through the 1952 season—and the last NFL team to do so—the single-wing offense featured four backs. These positions included a tailback, fullback, quarterback, and wingback. The single-wing employed a long snap from center, and the quarterback also served as a blocking back.

As a tailback during his Steelers days, Dudley took that direct snap, running downfield with success.

in a one-game playoff and lost 21–zip before a Forbes Field hometown crowd.

Too bad they didn't have Dudley to help.

In addition to his 1946 rushing title, he also led the NFL in punt returns (27 for 385 yards and a 14.3 average) and interceptions (10 for 242 yards and a 24.2 yard return average, including a touchdown). His lateral passing ability, an abandoned statistical record, also topped the NFL that year.

Statistically during the 1946 season, his last with the Pittsburgh Steelers (posting a 5–5–1 record), Dudley is listed in the team's passing, rushing, receiving, kick return, punt return, punting, kicking, and interception categories—in short, all of them.

Forget that he won the NFL's 1946 Joe F. Carr Trophy given to the MVP that year. Because of reputed difficulties and heated verbal exchanges with the Steelers head coach Jock Sutherland, Dudley would be traded to the Detroit Lions for the 1947 season.

During Dudley's nine NFL campaigns, he played with the Steelers, the Lions, and the Washington Redskins. The Pittsburgh legend was a 1966 Pro Football Hall of Fame inductee.

He did everything wrong. He couldn't throw. He was not fast. He was not big. He couldn't kick. But he led the league in ground gained and in interceptions. He was one of those players. Dudley was intelligent and explosive. He was a winner.

**—Dan Rooney commenting on "Bullet" Bill Dudley**

# FIRST OF TWO ONE-YARD BETTIS TOUCHDOWNS

Jerome Bettis's short touchdown runs topped off a 102-yard day for "the Bus" in an AFC wild-card victory over Indianapolis

**T**his playoff game started out as a grudge match that followed up on the previous year's AFC championship Steelers 20–16 win over the Indianapolis Colts. For at least the first half, the same wild momentum shifts held true. Something happened in the Indy locker room at halftime, though. They took the Three Rivers Stadium field in the third quarter unaware of the impending Black and Gold domination about to be unleashed.

Football is a great game for many reasons. Sometimes it all comes down to one yard. Three little feet can separate a team from a touchdown. Often that short run might even mean the difference between a win and a loss. A defensive stop and a field goal might be the only option if the team without the ball steps up and controls the line. The offense might fumble, throw an

A draft-day trade in 1996 sent Jerome Bettis from the Rams to the Steelers and rejuvenated the running back's career. In his first season in Pittsburgh, Bettis rushed for more than 1,000 yards, earned NFL Comeback Player of the Year honors, and led the Steelers to the playoffs. *AP Images*

interception, or even go for it on fourth down and fail. Gains for a yard mean everything.

Short touchdown runs in NFL history remain classics. Consider Baltimore Colts fullback Alan Ameche's one-yard run against the New York Giants to claim the 1958 league title in the "Greatest Game Ever Played." Certainly Green Bay Packers quarterback Bart Starr's one-yard game-winning quarterback sneak against the Dallas Cowboys in the 1967 NFL championship's "Ice Bowl" with 13 seconds remaining and minus-13-degree temperatures is a classic. There are others.

During his playing career, running back Jerome Bettis reigned as master of the short run. He'd do so twice in this big game. First the Steelers defense would beat up on the Colts a little, quarterback Jim Harbaugh in particular.

It all started innocently enough on this mild, 60°F, partly cloudy Pittsburgh football afternoon in late December. NFL referee Ed Hochuli, a trial lawyer off the field and muscular presence as on-field officials go, had things under control. That didn't stop the Steelers from inflicting some immediate in-your-face damage to their guests.

On the game's fifth play, Pittsburgh's Jason Gildon, a member of the Black and Gold linebacker corps, nailed Harbaugh. The aftermath found the former Chicago Bears quarterback with several chipped teeth and some chin stitches for his effort.

## JEROME BETTIS FACTS

Nicknamed "the Bus," Jerome Bettis was born in Detroit, Michigan, on February 16, 1972. Later that year, Franco Harris would make the Immaculate Reception on December 23, 1972.

Bettis, the 5'11" and 252-pound running back, attended the University of Notre Dame. The Rams, then based in Los Angeles, picked him in the 1993 NFL draft's first round. Bettis played 13 years in the NFL (1993–2005), his last 10 with the Steelers, retiring after Pittsburgh's amazing 2005 playoff run and victory in Super Bowl XL.

He ran for 13,662 yards during his career on 3,479 carries, averaging 3.9 per touch. He pounded out 91 rushing touchdowns. Bettis ran for more than 1,000 yards during eight different seasons. The Bus also caught 200 career passes for 1,449 yards (a 7.2 yard average) and three more touchdowns.

A six-time Pro Bowl player, his career reflects many honors and highlights: NFL Offensive Rookie of the Year (1993), three-time All-Pro, NFL Comeback Player of the Year (1996), Walter Payton Man of the Year (2001), and the Super Bowl XL win in his hometown. He was inducted into the Pro Football Hall of Fame in 2015.

# Game Details

## Pittsburgh 42 • Indianapolis 14

**Location:** Three Rivers Stadium, Pittsburgh, Pennsylvania

**Attendance:** 58,078

**Box Score:**

| | | | | | |
|---|---|---|---|---|---|
| **Colts** | 0 | 14 | 0 | 0 | **14** |
| **Steelers** | 10 | 3 | 8 | 21 | **42** |

*Scoring:*
PIT N. Johnson 29-yard FG
PIT Stewart 1-yard run (N. Johnson PAT)
PIT N. Johnson 50-yard FG
IND Daniel 59-yard interception return (Blanchard PAT)
IND Bailey 9-yard pass from Harbaugh (Blanchard PAT)
PIT Bettis 1-yard run (Farquhar pass from Stewart)
PIT Bettis 1-yard run (N. Johnson PAT)
PIT Witman 31-yard run (N. Johnson PAT)
PIT Stewart 3-yard run (N. Johnson PAT)

| Team | FD | RUSH | A-C-I | PASS |
|---|---|---|---|---|
| **Colts** | 8 | 15/41 | 33-13-1 | 105 |
| **Steelers** | 24 | 51/231 | 22-14-2 | 176 |

> I give him [Jim Harbaugh] lots of credit. It's my job to beat him up, but at the same time I have a lot of respect for him.
>
> **—Steelers linebacker Chad Brown**

Welcome to Three Rivers Stadium.

Enter another quarterback, former Harbaugh teammate with the Bears, Mike Tomczak. Both now veterans of the NFL wars, they'd duel with respective defenses during the game—that is, when other memorable plays weren't going on.

Norm Johnson got the Steelers on the board first with a 29-yard field goal. Kordell Stewart later added to these first quarter points with a one-yard run, and Johnson nailed the point after.

In the second quarter, Johnson continued his solid kicking with a 50-yard field goal, bringing to the score to Pittsburgh 13, Indy 0. And then things got interesting.

The Steelers and Tomczak had the ball at third-and-four on the Colts' 42-yard line and fewer than five minutes to go in the first half.

Maybe Pittsburgh got too comfortable. Maybe Tomczak telegraphed his intentions. On what appeared to be a short sideline pass to Ernie Mills, one that should have probably been safely lofted out of bounds,

## CHARLES EVERETT JOHNSON

For those Steelers fans who can't quite remember a Pittsburgh receiver named Charles Johnson, he was a first-round pick in the 1994 NFL draft.

Johnson, one of nine NFL players named Charles/Charley/Charlie with that same surname, played Steelers wideout for five seasons (1994–1998), completing his nine-year career with the Eagles, Patriots, and Bills.

He peaked in 1996, his third year, with 60 receptions for 1,008 yards, a solid 16.8 yards per catch, and three touchdowns. Johnson's longest reception in 1996 went for 70 yards. His 1998 season was solid, too, as he posted 65 catches, though for fewer yards (815).

As a Steelers rookie in 1994, he caught one for 84 yards, the longest in his career.

Colts cornerback Eugene Daniel stepped in and made the grab—and returned the prize 59 yards to the end zone.

And if this killjoy late-quarter turnover wasn't enough, Harbaugh would find a way to put another score on the board, a nine-yard touchdown pass to wideout Aaron Bailey, to boost the score to Colts 14, Steelers 13, following Indy's point after.

Not a good way for the Steelers to end the half.

Fortunately they started the second one like a different team.

On the opening drive of the third quarter, Pittsburgh put on a clinic for ball control, holding the pigskin for more than nine minutes. On those 16 well-conceived plays they covered 91 yards on a well-engineered drive. Enter Bettis, who took the last one of the drive into the end zone for a yard—the score to regain the squandered first-half lead. This big play, though short on yardage, turned momentum around and put it in the Steelers' favor.

Tight end John Farquhar caught the two-point conversion try. Now this game was going to be about points, and lots of them.

On a left-side blitz, Steelers safety Carnell Lake claimed a muffed pitchout to the Colts' Marshall Faulk, and Pittsburgh was back in business. Fans relish an opponent's turnover in moments like this. Following this gift grab, Bettis would run for another one-yard touchdown—his second of the day.

Kordell "Slash" Stewart made it fun with two more scores. The first saw him run 24 yards straight up the middle on a simple quarterback draw, then he got the ball to rookie running back Jon Witman (yet another Nittany Lions product, like Jack Ham and Franco Harris), who took it 31 yards for the score. The Steelers all-purpose player Stewart would add the final Pittsburgh touchdown of the day on a three-yard run.

As defense goes, Steelers linebacker Chad Brown (6'2", 245 pounds) would sack Harbaugh three times on the day. Along the way, Pittsburgh receiver Charles Johnson would pull in five receptions totaling 109 yards. Bettis would roll for 102 rushing—a football field more than his two big touchdowns.

Indianapolis never scored a second-half point.

# ANOTHER CLASSIC STEELERS COMEBACK

Steelers quarterback Kordell Stewart's simple but effective screen pass goes for a 41-yard gain, setting up the winning overtime kick

**M**aybe they should have given the game ball to New England Patriots quarterback Drew Bledsoe.

The Patriots racked up an early 14–0 lead in front of 60,013 fans at Foxboro Stadium in the town of Foxborough, Massachusetts—two correct but different spellings, mind you. Confused? That's okay, as the Steelers were unclear on the field too, at first. Things didn't look good. They needed a win to ensure the AFC Central Division title. To get it, they'd need to derail the New England offense and outfox the defense. In the end, the opposition's quarterback took care of the offense.

After a scoreless first quarter, New England put those 14 points on the board. Before halftime, Pittsburgh got seven points, finally scoring. Right after the break came three more for the Steelers— then three more early in the fourth quarter. As the

Steelers kicker Norm Johnson, No. 9, pumps his fist into the air after kicking the 31-yard game winner in overtime to beat the New England Patriots 24–21, as holder Mike Tomczak, No. 18, celebrates with him. *Getty Images*

## SOME KEY PLAYERS OF THE 1997 SEASON

In 1997 Kordell "Slash" Stewart completed 236 of 440 pass attempts for a 53.6 percentage and 3,020 yards. This included 21 touchdowns, 17 interceptions, and 12.8 yards per completion. His passer rating for 1997 sits at 75.2. Stewart also rushed for 476 yards on 88 touches and 11 touchdowns—the team's second leading rusher to Jerome Bettis.

Bettis ran for 1,665 yards—a career high—on 375 attempts and seven touchdowns that season. He finished second in the AFC to Terrell Davis's 1,750 rushing yards, and third overall in the NFL, as Barry Sanders ran for 2,053 that year.

Yancey Thigpen caught 79 passes for 1,398 yards, a 17.7 average, and seven touchdowns as well.

Norm Johnson, who clinched this big 24–21 win over the Patriots, went 40–40 on extra-point tries and 22–25 on field goals, registering 106 points during the 1997 season.

game entered its final moments, one point separated the teams: Patriots 14, Steelers 13. This was turning out to be quite a Saturday night.

The Steelers' momentum stalled when Patriots 5'7" and 190-pound running back Dave Meggett grabbed a deflected pass and scampered 49 big yards for the score: Patriots 21, Steelers 13.

And if the score wasn't bad enough, New England and their quarterback Bledsoe again had the ball with a little more than two minutes to go. Pittsburgh had no timeouts. Now at third-and-seven, the Patriots needed that first down. If they didn't get it, a punt might do the job, too.

They were denied both options.

Steelers defensive back Chris Oldham blitzed Bledsoe, who got that deer-in-the-headlights look. As the pressured quarterback attempted to connect with his man Meggett on a simple screen, big Pittsburgh defensive end Kevin Henry (6'4" and 282 pounds) stepped up and intercepted. If this drama wasn't enough, Henry ran for more than 30 yards and, once inside the red zone, lateraled the ball to fellow defensive line teammate Orpheus Roye. Roye ran it in for the score. Or did he?

Officials said otherwise and called it a forward lateral.

Fine. The Steelers were still down by eight, but Kordell Stewart had that confident swagger about him those days, and somehow he'd pull this out. Right?

Yes, even from a fourth-and-seven hole, he hit Yancey Thigpen on the sideline—first down. Could he? Would he? On third-and-goal, Stewart passed the ball to tight end Mark Bruener for the score.

Patriots 21, Steelers 19: two more points were needed for any shot at the potential overtime win.

Pittsburgh was not to be denied after all this drama. The Stewart-to-Thigpen magic continued as they connected on the pass reception for two points to tie at the end of regulation.

# Game Details

## Pittsburgh 24 • New England 21 (OT)

**Location:** Foxboro Stadium, Foxborough, Massachusetts

**Attendance:** 60,013

**Box Score:**

| Steelers | 0 | 7 | 3 | 11 | 3 | **24** |
|----------|---|---|---|----|---|--------|
| Patriots | 0 | 14 | 0 | 7 | 0 | **21** |

| Team | FD | RUSH | A-C-I | PASS |
|------|-----|-------|---------|------|
| Steelers | 22 | 40/138 | 48-26-2 | 266 |
| Patriots | 15 | 18/42 | 36-21-2 | 211 |

# THE ORIGINAL MULTIPURPOSE PLAYER

During his time with the Steelers (1995–2002), Kordell "Slash" Stewart made some major contributions as quarterback. He also ran the ball well. And caught his share of pass receptions. And he even punted. Still, the franchise's prototype for this sort of player came well before Stewart's time.

Enter John McNally, also known during his playing career as "Johnny Blood," a nickname creatively coined from the Rudolph Valentino film Blood and Sand. (McNally's buddy Ralph Hanson became "Ralph Sand.") A real character, as they say, McNally used both names to maintain college eligibility and play semipro football—not altogether uncommon in the 1920s: two names, same person.

He first played for the Milwaukee Badgers, Duluth Eskimos, and Pottsville Maroons. His best years came as a member of the Green Bay Packers, when he contributed to four championship seasons. He also took the field with Art Rooney's Pittsburgh (football) Pirates in 1934, 1937, and in 1938, his final season. McNally also served as player-coach for the Pirates from 1937 to 1939.

He could catch, run, pass, and punt—just like Stewart.

A member of the 1963 Pro Football Hall of Fame class, and as an example of his range, McNally led the 1937 Pirates in pass receptions with 10 for 168 yards (a 16.8 yard average) and four touchdowns. That season he also ran nine times for 37 yards and 4.1 yards per carry. In 1937 he also completed 10 passes for 115 yards and a touchdown. He returned a kickoff for a touchdown that year—the only one in the NFL that season. He also scored a defensive touchdown.

Okay, you get the idea.

Johnny Blood was Slash before anyone coined the nickname for Stewart.

Bill Dudley, another notable multipurpose player in the franchise's first two decades, played many positions for Pittsburgh in 1942, 1945, and 1946.

## TOP FIVE STEELERS PASS-COMPLETION LEADERS

1. Ben Roethlisberger (2004–present): 3,157 pass completions
2. Terry Bradshaw (1970–1983): 2,025 pass completions
3. Kordell Stewart (1995–2002): 1,190 pass completions
4. Neil O'Donnell (1990 draft choice; played 1991–1995): 1,069 pass completions
5. Bubby Brister (1986–1992): 776 pass completions

Good fortune continued in overtime as the Steelers won the coin toss. Bledsoe's botched screen had started this off, and Stewart's successful completion of such a play would turn events toward certain victory.

Stewart tossed an I'm-just-trying-to-gain-a-few-yards screen pass to wideout Courtney Hawkins—a Pittsburgh newcomer that season after five with Tampa Bay—who took it 41 yards downfield. Kicker Norm Johnson, almost always reliable in this kind of situation, booted the 31-yard game winner, pumping his right fist into the air as holder Mike Tomczak celebrated with him.

# BLEIER'S 27-YARD TOUCHDOWN CATCH

Rocky Bleier's touchdown catch led to a scoring outburst and a 1974 AFC divisional playoff win over the Buffalo Bills

**T**he box score makes you look twice.

With Christmas just three days away, in a long-ago time when the NFL playoffs arrived earlier than they do now—that is, the same year as the regular season—this Three Rivers Stadium home game started out innocently enough for the 48,321 fans in attendance. Truth is, some could have arrived late, left early, and still witnessed most of this playoff game's highlights.

All Steelers fans would soon get a holiday victory gift.

For starters, Pittsburgh's Roy Gerela chipped in a 21-yard first-quarter field goal for the matchup's first points. Little did he know the Steelers' kicking game would take a turn for the worse in the second quarter as the rest of the Black and Gold offense vigorously dominated the visiting Buffalo football team.

Steelers running back Rocky Bleier (No. 20) carries the football during the AFC divisional playoff victory over the Buffalo Bills on December 22, 1974, at Three Rivers Stadium. Bleier's 27-yard touchdown catch touched off the Steelers' 26-point second quarter. *Getty Images*

After Gerela's field goal, the Bills' quarterback, Joe Ferguson, hit his tight end Paul Seymour, a big target at 6′5″ and 252 pounds, for the first touchdown. The score was Buffalo 7, Pittsburgh 3 as the first quarter ended.

Watch enough game film of the 1970s Steelers teams, especially between the 1974 and 1979 seasons, and you'll see moments that defy possibility. You'll relive times when the Pittsburgh offense scored in a rapid-fire manner, running up points on the opponent. Such intervals thrilled fans. These spurts of flat-out dominance made it possible for the Steel Curtain to do its exceptional job and shut down offenses. This AFC matchup was no exception.

With Buffalo ahead by the score of 7–3, Terry Bradshaw hit Steelers running back Rocky Bleier for a 27-yard touchdown reception. It was the play Pittsburgh needed to get things rolling. Unfortunately, Gerela's point-after attempt was blocked.

Nevertheless, Pittsburgh kept gaining yards, unstoppable in that department. Next, Franco Harris scored on a one-yard touchdown run. The fans loved it—and Gerela, well…

He made his extra point.

Once again, and still in the second quarter, Pittsburgh drove downfield, relentless in its pursuit of another score. At the end of that effort, Harris ran four yards into the end zone for his next touchdown.

But look out…

Again, the Steelers kicker had his point-after try stifled. This was getting to be a bad habit.

Pittsburgh got the ball again as the Steel Curtain continued to shut the Bills out that quarter. Down the field came Bradshaw and Harris, who ran a yard for his third touchdown of the second quarter.

And, no lie, Mr. Gerela nailed the extra point. Miss. Make. Miss. Make. At least he was kicking .500.

Okay, a quick review: that's four second-quarter touchdowns—the Bleier scoring pass and three end-zone runs by Harris.

Most of this took place in 15 minutes of play. The Steelers' halftime lead settled in at 29–7.

As for the second half, O.J. Simpson would catch a three-yard Ferguson pass in the third quarter, and Gerela would provide a bookend field goal of 22 yards to put the last score of the day on the board in the fourth. Gerela's day's total: two for four on extra-point tries and two for two on field-goal attempts.

Hey, you can't have it all.

Pittsburgh would pile up 235 rushing yards on the day (51 attempts) and 203 passing for 438 total yards. Bradshaw completed 12 passes on 19 attempts with no interceptions. The Steelers would rack up 29 first downs.

# Game Details

## Pittsburgh 32 • Buffalo 14

**Location:** Three Rivers Stadium, Pittsburgh, Pennsylvania

**Attendance:** 48,321

**Box Score:**

| | | | | | |
|---|---|---|---|---|---|
| **Bills** | 7 | 0 | 7 | 0 | **14** |
| **Steelers** | 3 | 26 | 0 | 3 | **32** |

*Scoring:*
PIT Gerela 21-yard FG
BUF Seymour 22-yard pass from Ferguson (Leypoldt PAT)
PIT Bleier 27-yard pass from Bradshaw (Gerela PAT blocked)
PIT Harris 1-yard run (Gerela PAT)
PIT Harris 4-yard run (PAT blocked)
PIT Harris 1-yard run (Gerela PAT)
BUF Simpson 3-yard pass from Ferguson (Leypoldt PAT)
PIT Gerela 22-yard FG

| Team | FD | RUSH | A-C-I | PASS |
|---|---|---|---|---|
| **Bills** | 15 | 21/100 | 26-11-0 | 164 |
| **Steelers** | 29 | 51/235 | 21-12-0 | 203 |

# ROCKY BLEIER FACTS

A product of the University of Notre Dame with a degree in business management, running back Robert Patrick "Rocky" Bleier came to Pittsburgh as a 16th-round 1968 NFL draft pick.

In his 11 seasons, all with the Steelers (1968, 1971–1980), he rushed for 3,865 yards on 928 carries for a 4.2 average and 23 touchdowns. Bleier also caught 136 passes for 1,294 yards, a 9.2 average, and two touchdowns.

Drafted by the U.S. Army, Bleier was seriously wounded in Vietnam while on patrol and under ambush in August 1969. He was awarded both the Purple Heart and Bronze Star.

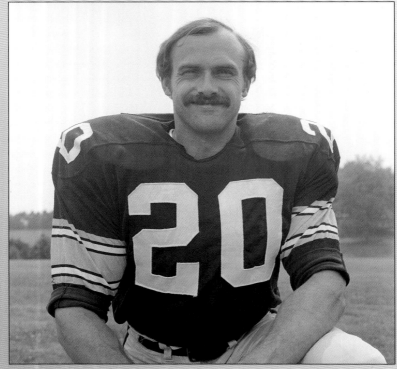

A preseason portrait of a smiling Rocky Bleier taken in August 1975. *AP Images*

After his return and recovery, Bleier was on the Pittsburgh Steelers injured reserve list in 1970. In 1971 he made the taxi squad, even appearing in six games. By 1972 he got on the active roster. In 1974 Bleier made the Steelers' starting backfield. During the 1976 season, Bleier ran for 1,036 yards on 220 carries for a 4.7 average.

He owns four Super Bowl rings and currently serves as president of Rocky Bleier, Inc. located in Pittsburgh.

The Steel Curtain would hold Simpson and company to 100 yards rushing and 164 passing. Ferguson threw 11 completions on 26 tries. Bills first downs totaled 15.

As for that wild quarter-by-quarter box score, it looked like this when the gun sounded—Bills: 7–0–7–0. Steelers: 3–26–0–3.

Crazy game. Big win.

# FINKS-TO-NICKEL PLAY-ACTION PASS

This infamous Jim Finks-to-Elbie Nickel touchdown pass ranked as the franchise's best play ever before the Immaculate Reception

**R**ivalries include dramatic wins and tough losses, a history of meetings and player matchups. Rivalries also feature in-your-face blocks and tackles, blood, sweat, and, earlier in this particular season, a Jim Finks broken jaw dished out by the Eagles in the Steelers' 24–22 loss to Philly during the third week of play.

You don't forget such a thing when your face still carries the roadmap of that encounter. If you were the Steelers quarterback and multipurpose player Mr. Finks, you likely wanted to dish out some revenge in the form of a win. And after all, these were two teams in the same state. Regional pride mattered.

There was the Steagles history in the days during World War II to consider, a merger of the two franchises as men served overseas—and the years that followed. Pittsburgh's first postseason

Forbes Field was the primary home of the Pittsburgh Steelers between 1933 and 1963. Here members of the visiting Chicago Bears shake hands with Steelers players on November 24, 1963. Final score: 17–17. President John F. Kennedy had been assassinated just two days before. *Photo Robert Riger/Getty Images*

appearance (a loss) came on Sunday, December 21, 1947, in the NFL Eastern Division championship against Philadelphia. The Steelers were shut out from scoring in every quarter as the Eagles club, with whom the Steelers teamed just years before, beat them 21–0.

That ranked as a big loss, as the next Steelers playoff appearance wouldn't follow until 25 years later.

These modern days, with the AFC Steelers only occasionally meeting up with the NFC Eagles, this interstate matchup and rivalry has pretty much dissolved into reflective memories of the old NFL by those who lived through it and remember. If you weren't around in

# JIM FINKS FACTS

The Steelers' Jim Finks spent seven years in the NFL as a player, primarily as a quarterback, but also as a defensive back and tailback, all with the Steelers (1949–1955).

As a quarterback, Finks completed 661 passes on 1,382 attempts during his career for a 47.8 passing percentage and 8,622 total yards, averaging 6.2 a toss. His longest pass completion went for 78 yards. These contributions mustered 55 touchdowns. He also rushed 118 times for 294 yards (2.5 yards per carry), his longest run going for 38 yards. Finks added 12 more touchdowns on runs, catching one pass as well for 17 yards and another touchdown during his playing career.

After his playing days, he successfully served as an NFL administrator with three teams—the Vikings, Bears, and Saints—making winners out of all three losing franchises.

Finks is a member of the 1995 Hall of Fame class for his influential administrative contributions.

October 1954 and haven't heard, here's what happened as the big Finks-Nickel play goes.

A then-Steelers record for Forbes Field attendance (39,075), fans did their best to provide 12th-man contributions from the stands, almost ensuring that this game would be memorable. It started off weaker, though, and you could have either called it a tough defensive struggle or a drought of offensive opportunity. In truth, it was both.

By halftime, Pittsburgh's kicker Ed Kissell—also listed as a defensive back in NFL histories and who played just two seasons with the Steelers (1952, 1954)—put the only points of the game on the board, a 24-yard field goal in the second quarter of play.

Score: Steelers 3, Eagles 0.

Something had to happen, as is often the case when defenses dominate. Some big play had to open things up, as the second half continued on like much of the first. Big hits. Bruising blocks. The score stayed the same.

Fourth-and–one, the Steelers had the ball on the Eagles' 40. Then and now, this speaks to a first-down necessity and likely a short run. Back then Pittsburgh fullback Jim Brandt (6'1" and 205 pounds) might get the call—though taller and lighter, he was the 1954 version of Jerome Bettis in short-yardage situations.

In this offensive series, Philly likely thought the same thing. Brandt. Handoff. Short run. Stop him.

Big plays rely on such predictable thinking, especially when they add a twist or two.

# Game Details

## Pittsburgh 17 • Philadelphia 7

**Location:** Forbes Field, Pittsburgh, Pennsylvania

**Attendance:** 39,075

**Box Score:**

| | | | | | |
|---|---|---|---|---|---|
| **Eagles** | 0 | 0 | 0 | 7 | **7** |
| **Steelers** | 0 | 3 | 7 | 7 | **17** |

*Scoring:*
PIT Kissell 24-yard FG
PIT Nickel 52-yard pass from Finks (Kissell PAT)
PHI Pihos 24-yard pass from Burk (Walston PAT)
PIT Chandnois 5-yard run (Kissell PAT)

| Team | FD | RUSH | A-C-I | PASS |
|---|---|---|---|---|
| **Eagles** | 15 | 30/121 | 34-18-2 | 157 |
| **Steelers** | 11 | 29/64 | 22-12-2 | 149 |

By definition, a play-action pass involves a quarterback (Finks) faking a handoff to a running back (Brandt) before throwing the ball to a receiver (Nickel). A play-action pass pretends that a running play is underway. It can be especially effective in a short-yardage situation, where the defense expects a handoff. It's got the same intentions as a flea-flicker but is less dangerous in execution because the ball isn't exchanged.

If effective, it fools the defense into defending the run, and the offense can capitalize on the error—especially if the defense is out of position for pass coverage.

As mentioned earlier, Pittsburgh was the last NFL team to employ the single-wing offense. By 1953, the season before this Finks-to-Nickel play-action pass, the Steelers franchise would switch to the T formation, which allowed the quarterback to take the snap from center and either hand the ball off or fake it, leading to an option play.

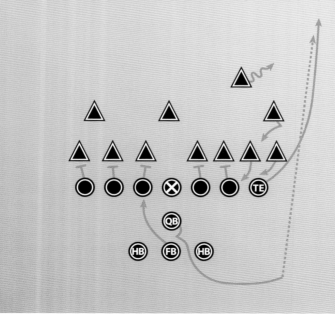

> The T shape commonly includes a halfback, fullback, and another halfback, in this offensive set, lined up behind the quarterback. Receiver variations include two tight ends or a tight end and a wide receiver. Again, in 1954, Nickel's position was simply called end—now it's tight end.
>
> Finks pulled off the sleight-of-hand move perfectly as his receiver drifted into the secondary, down the right sideline. Finks then got the ball to a wide-open Nickel.
>
> Touchdown Steelers.

Finks, of the broken jaw, called for the snap. Got the pigskin in his hands. Faked the football to his fullback Brandt, and of course, the Eagles bought it. Why not? The move seemed so obvious, a Philly defender's thought process might have played out... until it was too late.

A play-action pass is constructed to do just that: feign the apparent, fool the defense, and capitalize on their error. Finks pulled the magic trick off perfectly as Elbie Nickel drifted into the secondary like a player away from the play just might. The Steelers' quarterback settled in the pocket.

Philly defenders remained stalled out of position on their pass coverage. Finks swiftly hit the wide-open Nickel, who caught the ball and sprinted 40 yards untouched down the right sideline to daylight, putting Pittsburgh up 10–0.

The. Crowd. Went. Wild.

That's just one way to make a broken jaw feel better.

Following this great play, the Steelers held on to win 17–7 by the end of it, tying for first place in the Eastern Conference with a 4–1 record.

The play was the highlight of the 1954 season and years to follow. Pittsburgh would fade after this matchup and big win, losing six of their last seven games to go 5–7 on the season.

# THE BUS RIDES OVER CHICAGO

The Steelers won a snowy game against the Bears thanks largely to Jerome Bettis's unstoppable touchdown run over linebacker Brian Urlacher

**P**ittsburgh's 38–31 loss to the Bengals on December 4, 2005, had hurt. It had cost the Steelers the AFC Central division. It had left an impression.

And worse yet, on a gut-check level, Cincinnati's wideout T.J. Houshmandzadeh had even symbolized his team's victory over Pittsburgh by pretending to shine his shoes with a Terrible Towel, the symbol of Steelers pride. In the locker room, the orange, black, and white uniforms celebrated.

Annoying stuff. Fans didn't like it. The Steelers players surely didn't either. If anything, it likely fired up the Steelers for the following week.

Pittsburgh had now been on the losing side for three games in a row. After a strong start to the 2005 season, the numbers said everything:

Want old-school Steelers football played in the Heinz Field snow and mud? This one had it all, including Jerome Bettis's final 100-yard game in an incredible 13-year career. His performance helped salvage a season, and began Pittsburgh's eight-game winning streak and run to a Super Bowl XL victory. You could tell he enjoyed the moment. *Getty Images*

Steelers running back Jerome Bettis, No. 36, carries the football behind the block of guard Alan Faneca, No. 66. Chicago Bears linebacker Brian Urlacher, No. 54, awaits his fate as snow falls at Heinz Field on December 11, 2005. *Getty Images*

7–5. Would they even make the playoffs? The Steelers simply couldn't lose another game.

Their problem was that the best defense in football—the Chicago Bears'—was flying into Pittsburgh. One game only: a season on the line. If the Steelers won this one—a big if there—they'd have to follow up and prove themselves victorious in the next three games as well, just to make the playoffs.

No sixth-seeded team had ever reached the Super Bowl either, so that's what they had facing them. Again, though, the Black and Gold, as emphasized by their head coach Bill Cowher, were taking their schedule one game at a time.

Pittsburgh's December weather also arrived with the visiting Bears. Snow fell. Gray skies overhead darkened everything by the second half as twilight came on. The glare of the Heinz Field lights provided a gloomy look to the action, but things were actually looking brighter, figuratively speaking. The Steelers had come alive. They were playing like the team they had been before the losing streak and the winners they could be. It happened at just the right point during the season.

As Cowher later related in an NFL Films interview, he simply said to Jerome Bettis on the Pittsburgh sideline, "It's time," meaning No. 36 was going to get the ball and that the responsibility sat squarely on his big shoulders.

Pittsburgh was about to ride the Bus.

During the big game, Bettis churned up the middle on short runs, bulled through holes provided courtesy of the Steelers' offensive line, legged it for good yardage, snow falling all around, the No. 36 on the back of his uniform covered in mud. On many touches, he carried multiple Bears defenders on his back until they could drag him down. Twice they couldn't.

This was old-school Steelers football: run it up the gut and power out the win. This would also prove to be Bettis's final 100-yard game in an incredible 13-year career, and somehow you could just tell he was enjoying the moment.

On the most memorable play of this season-saving game, the Bus (along with the Wilson football) charged head-on into linebacker Brian Urlacher, the 6'4" and 258-pound play stopper. On impact the two players stalled—force meeting force, a bit like an auto accident to the viewer, one physical powerhouse intending to stop the runner, one vigorous body bent on running over the defender.

Urlacher's left knee caught Heinz Field turf as his right leg left the ground on impact. Collision insurance needed. Other Bears converged, but it was too late.

The 5'11" and 252-pound Bettis drove the Bears linebacker down, his left arm pushing into Urlacher, who fell backward just as the Bus ran over him.

The defender still desperately held on with his right arm, a reaching, grasping effort, struggling to hold No. 36. For a moment, that is.

Urlacher fell to the ground, flopped there, lying on his back, vanquished, as he watched Bettis bowl over him from the best seat in the house.

As several other Bears looked on, the Bus drove over the goal line.

Bettis's final game statistics read as a testament to weather-challenged football: 17 carries for 101 yards and two touchdowns. Solid. Successful. The score was Steelers 21, Bears 9. The best defense in football, the Chicago Bears, had taken a day off. In some ways, the Pittsburgh defense took over that title—at least on this day.

Pittsburgh would win the next seven games that followed, including Super Bowl XL.

# Game Details

## Pittsburgh 21 • Chicago 9

**Location:** Heinz Field, Pittsburgh, Pennsylvania

**Attendance:** 61,237

**Box Score:**

| | | | | | |
|---|---|---|---|---|---|
| **Bears** | 3 | 0 | 0 | 6 | **9** |
| **Steelers** | 7 | 7 | 7 | 0 | **21** |

*Scoring:*
PIT Ward 14-yard pass from Roethlisberger (Reed PAT)
CHI Gould 29-yard FG
PIT Bettis 1-yard run (Reed PAT)
PIT Bettis 5-yard run (Reed PAT)
CHI Jones 1-yard run (PAT failed)

| Team | FD | RUSH | A-C-I | PASS |
|---|---|---|---|---|
| **Bears** | 15 | 18/83 | 35-17-0 | 185 |
| **Steelers** | 20 | 46/190 | 20-13-0 | 173 |

# RUNAWAY BUS

Jerome Bettis bulldozed the Bears in the snow for 101 yards on 17 carries, and his most memorable play came when he ran over Brian Urlacher, Chicago's stalwart middle linebacker.

On a second-and-goal from the 5-yard line with less than six minutes to play in the third quarter, the line fired off the ball to the right with left guard Alan Faneca (66) and fullback Dan Kreider (35) pulling across the line of scrimmage. Bettis (36) ran behind right tackle where he met Urlacher (54), plowed through him, and scored to give the Steelers a commanding 21–3 lead.

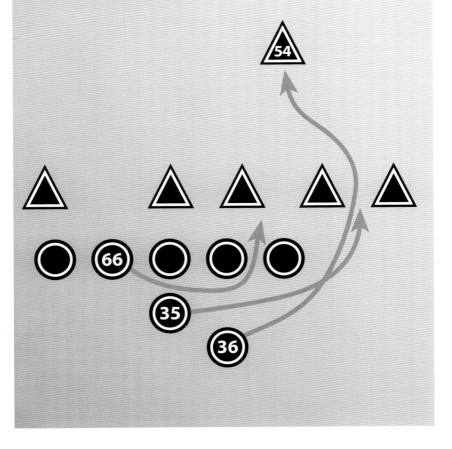

THE BEST
OFFENSE
IS A GOOD
DEFENSE

# TARKENTON TAKES A SAFETY

Dwight White's end-zone tackle in Super Bowl IX signaled the beginning of a Steelers dynasty

**F**or Black and Gold followers, Dwight White's defensive play was a hint of things to come.

The 80,997 fans attending that day—and those of us watching at home—did not see much in the way of first-half offense. Credit the drizzle and the New Orleans winter cold.

The game had originally been scheduled for the Louisiana Superdome, but construction on that facility wasn't completed so the venue became Tulane Stadium. Weather played a factor.

Pittsburgh had not won an NFL championship in all the years since Art Rooney's 1933 founding of the franchise. Things hadn't looked so good for changing that trend the week prior to the game. Steelers defensive end Dwight White, hospitalized just prior to Super Bowl IX, lost nearly 20 pounds during his bout with pneumonia. He wasn't even slated to play on this memorable winter's day.

Fran Tarkenton, Minnesota Vikings quarterback, scrambles after the loose ball that resulted in a safety during Super Bowl IX. This play provided the first Steelers points in an NFL Championship Game, and the first safety in Super Bowl history. *Getty Images*

But play he did. The actual safety went down like this.

Pittsburgh Steelers punter Bobby Walden, who had started his NFL career with the Minnesota Vikings, booted one into the wind and hung that ball end over end. It bounced after a fair catch had been called and was fielded on the 6-yard line. Minnesota was pinned deep.

Not good for them, but great for the Steel Curtain.

First down on Minnesota's 7-yard line. A simple handoff from Vikings quarterback Fran Tarkenton to running back Chuck Foreman yielded a three-yard gain for a bit of breathing room. In hindsight, maybe Minnesota should have stuck with Foreman on the second down. They didn't.

Vikings fullback Dave Osborn got the call on the next play and fumbled a frantic handoff from Tarkenton. (Some sources call it a pitch out, but I hold with the former after watching game film again.) Whether it was the Vikings quarterback's fault or the Minnesota running back's error, it's hard to tell. Either way, Osborn never got hold of the pigskin, and in the frenzy the ball was somehow bumped and booted back toward the end zone, bouncing away from the mad scrum just behind the line of scrimmage.

## STEEL CURTAIN FACTS

Though some fans have used the phrase to refer to the 1970s defensive line, still others dub the entire Steelers defense the Steel Curtain.

The well-known nickname was reportedly first generated by a WTAE radio station contest to name the Steelers defenders. The *Pittsburgh Post-Gazette* reported that Gregory Kronz was one of 17 listeners who submitted the nickname. A drawing determined the winner to be Kronz, a suburban ninth-grader at the time.

White, Ernie Holmes, Greene, and L.C. Greenwood formed the Steel Curtain's defensive line.

Defensive end White (1971–1980) was selected for the Pro Bowl in 1972 and 1973, though not during the seasons he earned four Super Bowl rings (IX, X, XIII, and XIV). White passed away on June 6, 2008.

Holmes (1972–1977), the other starting Steelers defensive tackle not named Joe Greene, won two Super Bowl rings with this defensive line. Released in 1978, he played three games that year with the New England Patriots before retiring. Holmes died in a car accident on January 17, 2008.

Greene, a Steelers defensive tackle from 1969 to 1981, is the only member of the defensive line in the Pro Football Hall of Fame.

Greenwood (1969–1981) played defensive end and, like Greene, made the NFL's 1970s All-Decade Team, which is elected by Hall of Fame voters. Greenwood passed away on September 29, 2013.

Free ball!

Now, fumbles on the playing field are one thing—even Foreman would fumble in the fourth quarter—but turnovers that roll in the direction of your own end zone are yet another. Such unexpected moments present immediate scoring opportunities for the defense.

# Game Details

## Pittsburgh 16 • Minnesota 6

**Location:** Tulane Stadium, New Orleans, Louisiana

**Attendance:** 80,997

**Box Score:**

| | | | | | |
|---|---|---|---|---|---|
| **Steelers** | 0 | 2 | 7 | 7 | **16** |
| **Vikings** | 0 | 0 | 0 | 6 | **6** |

*Scoring:*
PIT White downs Tarkenton for safety
PIT Harris 9-yard run (Gerela PAT)
MIN T. Brown recovered blocked punt in end zone (PAT failed)
PIT L. Brown 4-yard pass from Bradshaw (Gerela PAT)

| Team | FD | RUSH | A-C-I | PASS |
|---|---|---|---|---|
| **Steelers** | 17 | 57/249 | 14-9-0 | 84 |
| **Vikings** | 9 | 21/17 | 26-11-3 | 102 |

> Our attitude as a defense was that we would win this game 2-0.
>
> **—Andy Russell**

# STEELERS SHUT DOWN TARKENTON

Generously listed at 6' and 190 pounds, Francis Asbury Tarkenton had been tagged with the "Scramblin' Fran" nickname in the 1960s, as the elusive quarterback avoided sacks this fleet-cleated way. In 1969 he even published a book titled *Better Scramble Than Lose*, which somehow ironically foreshadowed the contrary outcome of Super Bowl IX.

Picked in the third round of the 1961 NFL draft, Tarkenton played for Minnesota (1961–1966), then the New York Giants (1967–1971), before returning to the Vikings for some of his best years (1972–1978).

By the time his career was said and done, Tarkenton would accrue 3,674 rushing yards plus 32 touchdowns on 675 carries. He also holds the distinction of running for touchdowns in 15 different seasons, an NFL record for quarterbacks. Such a reputation is not to be taken lightly in a Super Bowl game. The Steelers had faced one of Tarkenton's better Minnesota teams and beaten it.

Reputations matter, surely, but play execution is what wins games.

In the end, and here at the beginning of the 1970s Pittsburgh Steelers dominance, it's all about who has the most points on the board when time runs out. In Super Bowl IX, Tarkenton threw 26 times for 11 completions without turning a score. Moreover, three of his passes were intercepted. Many were hurried, and four were deflected.

Cat-quick, Tarkenton scrambled toward the ball and dove on it, sacrificing two points for a possible six before the point-after attempt. Right place, right time: White claimed those two "team safety" points for the Steelers. To be honest, it was more like a simple two-hand-touch tag game, as White quickly converged on the fetal-positioned Tarkenton and reached down to touch him with both hands.

A simple football move, yes. A lackluster play for some, no doubt. But it was a huge factor in this particular game.

White had jump-started the next phase of Steelers football history, as had the rest of the Steel Curtain defense. Dynasty teams must have player depth, and the Black and Gold had that. Even Pittsburgh backup linebackers Ed Bradley and Loren Toews deserve notice, as they replaced injured starters Andy Russell and Jack Lambert for much of the second half.

Solid defense makes good offense possible. Running back Franco Harris would be named the game's MVP, rushing for 158 yards on 34 attempts, his longest dash going 25, with one touchdown. The Steelers put up 333 yards of total offense.

Pittsburgh Steelers running back Franco Harris (32) and defensive tackle Joe Greene carry head coach Chuck Noll off the field after the 16–6 win over the Minnesota Vikings in Super Bowl IX. *Getty Images*

Thanks to White and the mighty Steel Curtain defense, the Vikings offense never scored a point, and only Minnesota's defense put six on the board after a blocked punt in the end zone. Even Minnesota's point-after attempt spluttered. The Steelers defense, including White, held the Vikings to only 17 rushing yards, 119 yards of total offense, and nine first downs.

High-fives to the Pittsburgh defense in general, and defensive end White in particular, for putting the Super Bowl's first safety on the

## POP CULTURE AND SUPER BOWL IX

As pop culture goes, this game provided an early example of multimedia interest in the Super Bowl. The night before Super Bowl IX, CBS's The Mary Tyler Moore Show, set in Minneapolis, Minnesota, incorporated the game in its plotline. In this episode, character Lou Grant teaches Ted Baxter about football betting, indicating he'll use Baxter's money and his own to bet on the Minnesota Vikings to win the game, which in this fictional sitcom, they do. The inevitable plot twist? Later in the televised broadcast, and much to Ted's disappointment, it's revealed that instead of sticking to the plan, Lou bet all the cash on the Steelers.

As post-episode credits rolled, actor Mary Tyler Moore offered this disclaimer: "If the Pittsburgh Steelers win the actual Super Bowl tomorrow, we want to apologize to the Pittsburgh team and their fans for this purely fictional story." She concluded by saying, "If, on the other hand, they lose, remember you heard it here first."

Super Bowl IX ticket.
*Getty Images*

Z 68 50
SEC. ROW SEAT

SUPER BOWL
IX

Sunday, January 12, 1975
Kickoff 2:00 P.M.    $20.00
all taxes included
AFC-NFC World Championship Game
Sunday, January 12, 1975    Kickoff 2:00 P.M.
Tulane Stadium, New Orleans, Louisiana    $20.00

OS 68 Z
SEC. ROW SEAT

board, the only points of the first half, and the first Steelers points in an NFL championship game—a memorable score on the way toward the Steelers' and Rooney's first Super Bowl win.

Head coach Chuck Noll was carried off the field on the shoulder pads of Harris and Joe Greene. Team captain, linebacker Russell, presented the game ball to "the Chief," Rooney.

It's also somehow fitting that this would be the last of three Super Bowls held at Tulane Stadium—the last professional game ever held there, for that matter—as it was demolished five years later.

An aerial view of Tulane Stadium in New Orleans, site of Super Bowl IX. *Getty Images*

# DOWN GOES PALMER

Steelers nose tackle Kimo von Oelhoffen rolls into the Bengals quarterback and changes the face of a wild-card game

**D**uring the 2005 regular season the Cincinnati Bengals had claimed the top AFC North spot over Pittsburgh. Marvin Lewis, hired as head coach in 2003, had just returned the Bengals to the playoffs for the first time since the 1990 team pulled a 41–14 wild-card win over the Houston Oilers. Carson Palmer had also recently fired up his offense behind some no-huddle assertiveness, a flash of offensive potential, surely.

Now the Paul Brown Stadium crowd wanted playoff blood.

Despite their regular-season road win over Pittsburgh back on December 4, 2005, by a score of 38–31, Cincinnati had drifted unmoored into the playoffs with two losses to close things out. On the other hand, the Steelers had steamrolled to four wins in a row after their regular-season defeat by Palmer's team, posting an 11–5 record— the same as the Bengals.

And that's what leads us to our next memorable moment, or rather what scene remained

Cincinnati quarterback Carson Palmer had just completed the longest pass in Bengals playoff history, a 66-yard toss to Chris Henry. Away from the action, Palmer writhed on the field. The play changed the game. *Getty Images*

after one impressive pass completion early in the game. The play itself started out simply enough: Bengals quarterback Palmer stood tall and ready in the pocket, looking downfield as rookie receiver Chris Henry tried to free himself from Pittsburgh defenders and get open for a pass.

An NFL quarterback's mental tenacity of hanging tough as defenders swarm across the line of scrimmage is often the difference between a good quarterback and a mediocre one, a starter and bench-sitter. Palmer hung in there just one second longer.

That second would cost the Bengals the season.

Surely and swiftly Henry got open on the right sideline, streaking downfield. The ball followed directly, a laser beam to cut the Steelers to the quick. Completion. The 66-yard catch, Cincinnati's first pass of the game, established itself as the best in Bengals playoff history, here in their first postseason appearance in 15 years. It was highlight-reel worthy, but to say it was bittersweet is something of an understatement.

Away from the downfield action, Kimo von Oelhoffen, the Steelers' 6'4", 300-pound nose tackle who had spent his first half-dozen seasons on the Cincinnati roster, started toward, then rolled into Palmer. The big defender's momentum carried his shoulder into the quarterback's left leg. That knee bent inward. Palmer folded, dropped. The Paul

## MOMENTUM CHANGER

The Bengals seemed to rally at the loss of their quarterback Palmer—at least in the first half. Maybe it was the veteran Jon Kitna's resolute rise to the occasion. Cincinnati led 10–zip at the first quarter's end, and the Bengals were up 17–14 by the time both teams retreated to their respective locker rooms. You could almost feel the Steelers readying for a second-half push.

Sure enough, in the third quarter, Jerome Bettis ran five yards for a score, and Jeff Reed's point after added to the lead: Steelers 21, Bengals 17. And then came the trick play that sealed the deal.

Pittsburgh Steelers wide receiver Antwaan Randle El took a direct snap. Randle El lateraled the ball to Pittsburgh quarterback Roethlisberger. By then Steelers wide receiver Cedrick Wilson was downfield, and they connected for a 43-yard pass reception and touchdown. It was a warm-up for the crucial gadget play to come later in Super Bowl XL.

Pittsburgh would put a field goal on the board in the fourth quarter, and Cincinnati would score no points that second half.

At the start of the 2006 NFL season, after months and months of rehab, his knee surgically repaired by using the Achilles' tendon of a woman killed by a drunk driver, Palmer would be back on the playing field.

Von Oelhoffen would be too, but with the New York Jets.

Brown Stadium crowd of 65,870, who had roared at the pass reception, went silent. Shocked, they looked on. A grim quiet filled the stadium as their quarterback writhed on the field.

Forget that Palmer had been wearing a protective brace on his left knee since the tail end of the 2004 season, when he sprained it. Ligaments were now torn. Cartilage damaged. Even Palmer's kneecap was dislocated. Not a pretty sight.

A gurney wheeled Cincinnati's hopes off the field.

# Game Details

## Pittsburgh 31 • Cincinnati 17

**Location:** Paul Brown Stadium, Cincinnati

**Attendance:** 65,870

**Box Score:**

| | | | | | |
|---|---|---|---|---|---|
| **Steelers** | 0 | 14 | 14 | 3 | **31** |
| **Bengals** | 10 | 7 | 0 | 0 | **17** |

*Scoring:*
CIN Graham 23-yard FG
CIN Johnson 20-yard run (Graham PAT)
PIT Parker 19-yard pass from Roethlisberger (Reed PAT)
CIN Houshmandzadeh 7-yard pass from Kitna (Graham PAT)
PIT Ward 5-yard pass from Roethlisberger (Reed PAT)
PIT Bettis 5-yard run (Reed PAT)
PIT Wilson 43-yard pass from Roethlisberger (Reed PAT)
PIT Reed 21-yard FG

| Team | FD | RUSH | A-C-I | PASS |
|---|---|---|---|---|
| **Steelers** | 19 | 34/144 | 21-14-0 | 202 |
| **Bengals** | 19 | 20/84 | 41-25-2 | 243 |

# THE ZONE BLITZ

Developed by Steelers defensive coordinator Dick LeBeau—a one-time Detroit Lions defensive back himself (1959–1972)—and dubbed "Blitzburgh" in its application, the system begins with the 3-4 defense.

Trading typical 3-4 lineman and even linebacker pressure on the quarterback for defensive blitzing force now applied by cornerbacks and safeties, LeBeau confused offensive lines with this harassment scheme.

As a result, defensive position players who would typically cover offensive receivers now blitzed, while linebackers—even defensive linemen—dropped back to cover pass attempts.

Other NFL defensive coordinators have since adopted LeBeau's innovative package, and why not? It works.

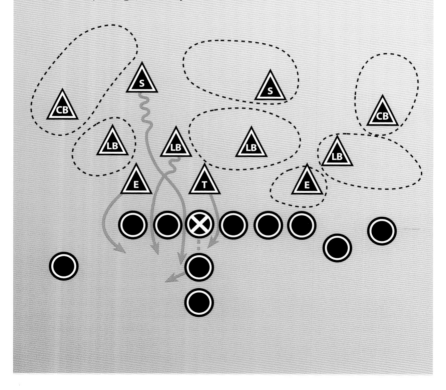

Palmer later said, "I knew right away it was bad. I felt my whole knee pop. I didn't feel a lot of pain. It was just a sickening feeling because I knew what it was and that my season was over."

Instantly Steelers and Bengals fans alike realized what had happened. To ignore that such an event played a factor in Pittsburgh's amazing run to Super Bowl XL would be dishonest. As unfortunate as the circumstances were, it gave the Black and Gold an edge. Once underdogs, it now looked like Coach Cowher and company might have some hope.

Responses to the season-ending injury varied. Bengals players voiced their on-field frustration directly at von Oelhoffen, who later said, "They had every right to be upset. They lost their best player. I hope Carson gets better. My apologies to him and his family."

The Bengals right tackle Willie Anderson said, "Guys were infuriated, but I know him [von Oelhoffen]. He's not a dirty player. His momentum just kept him going into Carson. It wasn't a dirty play." As further evidence, the nose tackle wasn't penalized for the hit.

Ironically, wide receiver Henry hurt his knee on the record pass from Palmer, then aggravated that injury not long after, and spent the second half on crutches.

Though backup Bengals quarterback Jon Kitna did what he could—24 completions on 40 attempts for 197 yards, a touchdown and two interceptions—in the end it was not enough. Roethlisberger went 14 for 21 and got 208 well-managed passing yards, three touchdowns, and no interceptions.

In this game played on the road, like those in Indianapolis and Denver in the following weeks, the Bengals, Colts, and Broncos seemed to have a home field disadvantage.

The 3-4 Defense: three down linemen, four linebackers (two outside and two inside), and four traditionally set defensive backs. This defensive scheme is often employed in a first-and-10 situation. Head coach Chuck Noll and the Steelers first used the 3–4 in 1983. Prior to this, the 4-3 defense was in place during the Steel Curtain era. Bill Cowher continued using the 3-4 when he took the reins in 1992. Former defensive coordinator Dick LeBeau favored it, and Pittsburgh has built a roster around this base defense in which a trio of linemen (and the four linebackers) pressure quarterbacks.

Dime: four down linemen (two are linebackers), one middle linebacker, and six defensive backs. The dime suits a likely passing situation, say third-and-10 or third-and-long. Offenses, however, can sometimes exploit the dime by running the ball.

### 3–4 DEFENSE

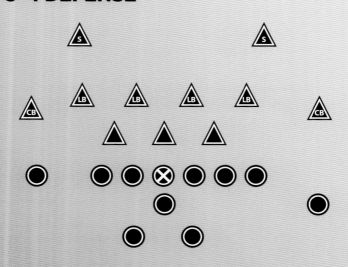

Nickel: four down linemen (again, two are linebackers), plus two inside linebackers and five defensive backs. Like the dime, the nickel is intended to defend the pass, but it provides enough punch to stop the run as well. It often suits second- and third-down matchups. The 2003 season dusted off and introduced the nickel as a primary Pittsburgh defensive package for flexibility.

Down and distance influence employment of the 3–4, dime, and nickel. Steelers linebackers play major roles as pressure defense pass rushers, run stoppers, and as drop-back pass defenders.

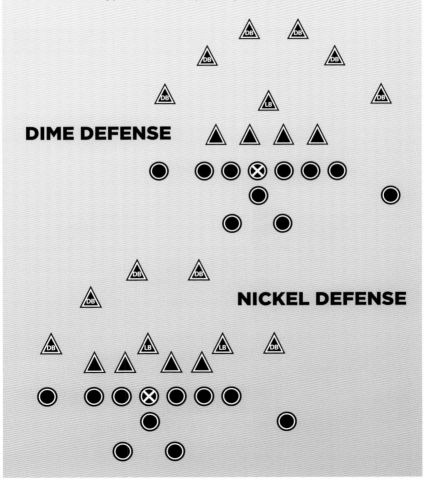

DIME DEFENSE

NICKEL DEFENSE

# RUSSELL'S FUMBLE RECOVERY AND TOUCHDOWN RUN

Linebacker Andy Russell's big play after Jack Ham forced a fumble clinched a 1975 AFC divisional playoff win

**S**ure, New York Giants linebacker Lawrence Taylor could apply defensive aggression better than most. The Chicago Bears' wide-eyed and intense Mike Singletary could stare down quarterbacks and also motivate his defense with the best of them. Bears legend Dick Butkus was a tenacious tackler and feared by offenses. The late great Packer Ray Nitschke could hit as hard as a heavyweight boxer. Many great linebackers played this game, including two on the Pittsburgh Steelers roster at the time: Jack Lambert and Jack Ham.

None of them ever managed what Andy Russell did on this day.

The play came in the fourth quarter, with the Colts deep in Steelers territory. A seven-time Pro Bowl player, veteran linebacker Russell was playing in his next-to-last season, a dozen all told. You need that sort of guy to put a stop to the opposition's efforts to get back in the game. Like Taylor, Singletary, Butkus, and Nitschke, Russell had that innate desire to seize opportunities and get the offense back on the field.

On this occasion he created a point-producing highlight of his own.

You have to wonder, in such instances, if these stalwart NFL defensive types don't take just a little pleasure in getting their hands on the football and actually running downfield with it, sometimes even for a score.

Andy Russell's fumble recovery and 93-yard touchdown run after linebacker Jack Ham forced the ball from Colts quarterback Bert Jones still ranks right up there as a greatest play in franchise history. *Getty Images*

# NFL FUMBLE HISTORY Q&A

Quarterbacks, who handle the football more than anyone on the NFL playing field, possess game, season, and career fumble records. Quarterback Bert Jones's fumble made Russell's run-back possible. Here's some NFL history on losing possession of the ball by fumbling it.

Who has fumbled the most times in an NFL game? Kansas City Chiefs quarterback Len Dawson has, seven times, while playing the San Diego Chargers on November 15, 1964. Dawson, incidentally, saw limited playing time during his first three NFL seasons with the Steelers (1957–1959).

Who fumbled the most times in a season? It's a tie. Kerry Collins (2001) and Daunte Culpepper (2002) each fumbled 23 times.

Who recovered the highest number of his own fumbles in a game? Randall Cunningham, Joe Ferguson, Roman Gabriel, Sam Etcheverry, and Otto Graham all hold this record, having recovered four of their own fumbles.

Who recovered the highest number of his own fumbles in a season? David Carr recovered the most, with an even dozen.

Who fumbled the most times in his NFL career? Brett Favre did, with 166.

Who snatched up the most opponent fumbles in a season? Don Hultz did, with nine.

Who forced the most career fumbles? Derrick Thomas forced 45.

Who recovered the highest number of opponents' fumbles in his career? Jim Marshall got 29.

How many individual players have gained the record number of opponent fumble recoveries in a single game? Fifteen total players have grabbed the ball three times each.

Who has returned the highest number of fumbles for touchdowns? Jason Taylor, with six.

What is the longest fumble return for a touchdown? It's 104 yards, and two players hold the record: Jack Tatum and Aeneas Williams.

Linebacker Andy Russell's fumble recovery and 93-yard touchdown run after Jack Ham forced the ball from quarterback Bert Jones still ranks right up there in the hearts of Steelers fans who saw it.

Pittsburgh Steelers linebacker Joey Porter forces a fumble off Cleveland Browns quarterback Tim Couch during the fourth quarter on November 11, 2001, at Cleveland Browns Stadium. Pittsburgh defeated Cleveland 15–12 in overtime. *Getty Images*

The integrity of the Steel Curtain defense made such plays possible, especially the talent of Dwight White, Ernie Holmes, Joe Greene, and L.C. Greenwood. This front four's steady aggression enabled the Steelers linebackers to play pass defense so effectively. This front four also made Russell's fumble recovery and score possible.

Down 10–7 at one point, Pittsburgh fought back to establish a 21–10 lead. Anyone who watches football knows an 11-point advantage can evaporate faster than you can speed dial home-delivery pizza and pay for it at your door.

Bert Jones, who had just returned to the game at the start of the fourth quarter after a first-half injury, established an Indianapolis Colts drive that had his team on the Steelers' 3-yard line. The game suddenly gave fans that uneasy feeling of a turnaround in the making.

# Game Details

## Pittsburgh 28 • Baltimore 10

**Location:** Three Rivers Stadium, Pittsburgh, Pennsylvania

**Attendance:** 49,557

**Box Score:**

| | | | | | |
|---|---|---|---|---|---|
| **Colts** | 0 | 7 | 3 | 0 | **10** |
| **Steelers** | 7 | 0 | 7 | 14 | **28** |

*Scoring:*
PIT Harris 8-yard run (Gerela PAT)
BAL Doughty 5-yard pass from Domres (Linhart PAT)
BAL Linhart 21-yard FG
PIT Bleier 7-yard run (Gerela PAT)
PIT Bradshaw 2-yard run (Gerela PAT)
PIT Russell 93-yard fumble recovery return (Gerela PAT)

| Team | FD | RUSH | A-C-I | PASS |
|---|---|---|---|---|
| Colts | 10 | 41/82 | 22-8-2 | 72 |
| Steelers | 16 | 43/211 | 13-8-2 | 76 |

And that's when one of the two Jacks, Ham in this case, got involved, sacking the drive out of Jones and forcing a fumble in the process. Russell scooped up that free pigskin at the 7-yard line and jogged, loped, and lumbered his way 93 yards for a touchdown. Ever eager to administer hard-hitting pain, White, Donnie Shell, and other members of the Steelers defense kept the converging Colts off their man Russell.

The Steelers defense held Baltimore to 154 total yards during the game. Though both teams completed only eight passes each, running back Franco Harris rushed for 153 yards himself—one less than the Colts' production. As Russell has said of the Steel Curtain defense, "We believed we could take the ball away from the offense ourselves and score."

And so they did.

## ANDY RUSSELL FACTS

Drafted in the 16th round by the Steelers in 1963 (there were just 14 teams in the NFL at the time), Russell signed with Pittsburgh. His salary? Meager by today's standards: $12,000, plus a $3,000 signing bonus.

The 6'2" and 225-pound linebacker played his rookie season, making the All-Pro Rookie Team that year. He then served in the military overseas in Germany (1964, 1965). Russell returned to the Steelers in 1966.

He also attended graduate school in the off-season, earning an MBA in finance from the University of Missouri in 1967. He started his own company, and to this day he remains a successful businessman.

In 1971 he was named Steelers MVP. Russell was also elected to the NFL's All-Decade Team (1965–1975).

The Steelers team captain for 10 seasons, he retired with two Super Bowl rings (1974, 1975). Russell opts to wear the first one on his hand, though he's proud of both.

Known for his altruistic efforts, he created the Andy Russell Charitable Foundation in 1999 to contribute to children's charities.

# ERNIE STAUTNER'S PUNISHING PAYBACK

A hard-nosed tackle forces third-string quarterback and future Dallas Cowboys coach Tom Landry out of the game

It was week 10 of the 12-week 1952 NFL season, the Sunday following Thanksgiving. It was a different time, both for the United States and for the Pittsburgh Steelers. The Korean War was ongoing, and polio was still a serious threat to the nation's health. Sports, as always, provided some relief, and this game was no exception. Steelers head coach Joe Bach and his team would go on to post a 5–7 record this season, finish fourth in the American Conference, and fail to make the playoffs—nothing new to Pittsburgh football fans during this era in franchise lore. Still, there were notable highlights along the way.

As of 1952 Pittsburgh was the last NFL team to employ the single-wing offense. In this set invented by Glenn "Pop" Warner, a direct snap from center is used, often made directly to the fullback or tailback, and yes, the quarterback as well. The formation includes a quarterback,

Ernie Stautner played defensive tackle, for which he was best known, but also defensive end and even offensive guard. He would eventually be named to nine Pro Bowls during his 14-year career, and the NFL's All-Decade Team of the 1950s. *Getty Images*

tailback, fullback, and wingback. The offensive line is intentionally off-balance, with four linemen on one side of the center and two on the other. Some say it resembles a wing, from which it gets its name.

Losing teams like the 1952 Steelers must change to win—or at least attempt to adopt new strategies. So, by 1953 the Steelers franchise would switch to the T formation, which allowed the quarterback to take the snap from center and either hand the ball off or fake it, leading to an option play. The T shape commonly includes a halfback, fullback, and another halfback in this offensive set, lined up behind the quarterback. Receiver variations include two tight ends or a tight end and a wide receiver.

As a result of this change, the Steelers and Bach would earn one more win in the 1953 campaign, going 6–6 to break even.

The November 30, 1952, game involved two future Hall of Fame players, one who would later be inducted primarily for his role as a player (though he would coach on many teams), Steelers defensive tackle Ernie Stautner (1950–1963). Another major figure also played in

## OTHER STAUTNER FACTS

Born April 20, 1925, in Prinzing-by-Cham, Bavaria, Germany, Stautner and his family emigrated to the United States, and East Greenbush, New York (near Albany), when Stautner was three years old.

He later served as a United States Marine before attending Boston College, where he earned a bachelor's degree in psychology (1950).

The Steelers picked up Stautner in the NFL draft's second round. He played his entire 14-year career with the Pittsburgh Steelers and was an assistant coach with the Steelers (1963, 1964) and then the Washington Redskins (1965).

He was inducted into the Pro Football Hall of Fame on September 13, 1969, in his first year of eligibility.

A member of Landry's coaching staff, Stautner served as the Dallas Cowboys defensive line coach (1966–1972) and defensive coordinator (1973–1988). In 1988 and 1989, he scouted for the Cowboys.

He was also head coach of the Dallas Texans arena football team (1990) and defensive line coach of the Denver Broncos (1991–1994) under both Dan Reeves and Wade Phillips.

He clearly lived for football, returning to his country of birth to become head coach of NFL Europe's Frankfurt Galaxy for three years, leading them to two consecutive World Bowls (1995, 1996) and winning the first one.

Stautner passed away on February 16, 2006, at age 80. He was posthumously elected to the Steelers' 75th-Anniversary All-Time Team in November 2007.

Dallas Cowboys defensive coordinator Ernie Stautner coaches his players during a game against the Pittsburgh Steelers at Three Rivers Stadium on November 20, 1977. The Steelers beat the Cowboys 28–13. *Getty Images*

this game, but he would later be better known for his coaching expertise. That guy was Tom Landry.

A lanky 6'1" and 195 pounds, Landry played the multiple roles of quarterback, halfback, defensive back, and even punter during his playing career with the New York Football Yankees (All-America Football Conference, 1949) and the New York Giants (NFL, 1949–1955). Though he had been taken in the 20th round of the draft, he counted

# Game Details

## Pittsburgh 63 • Giants 7

**Location:** Forbes Field, Pittsburgh, Pennsylvania

**Attendance:** 15,140

**Box Score:**

| Giants | 0 | 0 | 7 | 0 | **7** |
|---|---|---|---|---|---|
| **Steelers** | 14 | 14 | 7 | 28 | **63** |

*Scoring:*

PIT Chandnois 91-yard kickoff return (Kerkorian PAT)
PIT Chandnois 5-yard run (Kerkorian PAT)
PIT Nickel 21-yard pass from Finks (Kerkorian PAT)
PIT Mathews 42-yard pass from Finks (Kerkorian PAT)
PIT Hensley 25-yard pass from Finks (Kerkorian PAT)
NY Stribling 55-yard run with lateral from Scott after 15-yard
   pass from Landry (Poole PAT)
PIT Hensley 60-yard pass from Finks (Kerkorian PAT)
PIT Hays 3-yard blocked punt return (Mathews PAT)
PIT Butler 20-yard pass from Kerkorian (Kerkorian PAT)
PIT Modzelewski 3-yard run (Kerkorian PAT)

| Team | FD | RUSH | A-C-I | PASS |
|---|---|---|---|---|
| Giants | 8 | 20/15 | 39-11-7 | 147 |
| Steelers | 20 | 35/123 | 31-15-3 | 292 |

a 40.9 punting average and 32 career interceptions as a defensive back among his individual player accomplishments. As the Giants' player-coach in 1954 and 1955, Landry would develop his talent before becoming the full-time defensive coach from 1956 to 1959. Starting with the 1960 NFL season, Landry became head coach of the Dallas Cowboys and remained so for 29 campaigns, winning 13 divisional championships and two Super Bowl victories in five appearances. Two of those losses came against the Steelers.

But this was November 1952, and all those achievements would come later. On the other side of the line stood Stautner, 6'1" and 230 pounds of Pittsburgh Steeler.

As a Boston College footballer, Stautner lined up as both offensive and defensive tackle. In the NFL Stautner played defensive tackle, for which he was best known, but also defensive end, and even offensive guard. He would eventually be named to nine Pro Bowls during his 14-year career, and the NFL's All-Decade Team of the 1950s.

Stautner had that look that said, "This is a football player." Rugged. Mobile. A resilient lineman, he missed just six games in his NFL career because of injuries: broken ribs, broken hands, and an injured shoulder and nose. Opportunistic with offensive errors, Stautner also recovered 23 fumbles by opponents during his career, along with claiming three safeties, a record at the time.

On this cold and snowy day, some 15,140 Forbes Field fans saw the Steelers start fast. Offensive threat Lynn Chandnois ran the first kickoff back for a touchdown. A penalty nullified it. Undaunted, he ran the next kick back 91 yards for a score. It was going to be that kind of day for the Giants.

The defense, led by Stautner, tackled, clawed, and crushed the Giants offense, picking seven interceptions out of the air. Along the way Pittsburgh ran up the score, primarily on the back of Jim Finks, who would throw 12 for 24, four of those passes for touchdowns, and 254 yards all told.

New York would only eke out 15 rushing yards.

This sort of rout was rare for the Pittsburgh Steelers. In fact, it's the highest game score ever posted by the franchise.

# LANDRY'S 4-3 DEFENSE

The 4–3 defensive alignment, popularized by Landry during his time as the Giants defensive coordinator, includes four down linemen (two on each side of the offensive center), three linebackers (left, middle, and right), two cornerbacks on each side to cover wide receivers, and two safeties.

Landry, of course, is best known for his 29-season tenure with the Dallas Cowboys (1960–1988), during which he won two Super Bowls (VI, 1971 season; XII, 1977 season).

Pittsburgh's Steel Curtain of the 1970s and early 1980s played the 4-3 with obvious success (four Super Bowl wins). After his hiring as head coach beginning with the 2007 season, much media attention focused on Mike Tomlin's preference for the 4-3, though the 3-4, dime, and nickel schemes have been recent Steelers defensive-set preferences. Roster personnel and matchups determine defensive schemes. Time will tell.

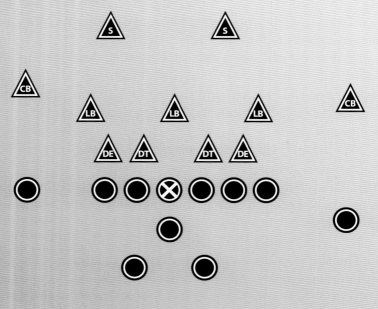

Maybe the Giants were looking for something, anything, when they passed and lateraled their way to New York's only score. But that wouldn't be the last Landry and company would hear from Stautner, who tackled the Giants quarterback and future coach, putting him on the sideline and out of the game.

And that's just one example of why Stautner's No. 70 jersey is one of only two numbers the Steelers have ever officially retired. He'd be named to the Pro Bowl for the first time that 1952 season, an honor followed by many more.

In the end Landry wouldn't hold the pounding tackle against Stautner, as years later they coached the Dallas Cowboys together.

Pittsburgh Steelers defensive tackle Gene "Big Daddy" Lipscomb shared the front line with Ernie Stautner during the 1961 and 1962 NFL seasons. Here Lipscomb rushes Dallas Cowboys quarterback Eddie LeBaron. *Getty Images*

# ERIC WILLIAMS INTERCEPTS

With the AFC divisional playoff game tied, the Steelers' interception of John Elway sets up the winning touchdown

**E**ric Williams—three played by that name in the NFL, and there was even an Erik Williams in the mix, making it four—came to the Steelers as a sixth-round pick out of North Carolina State University in the 1983 draft. A 6'1" and 188-pound defensive back, he'd play just five years in the NFL (1983–1987) and just four of them with Pittsburgh. His interception proved crucial in this big playoff game.

In 1983 the Steelers were slipping, trying to hold on to the legacy that had ruled the 1970s. Four Super Bowl victories established the franchise as a true dynasty.

Not lately, though. While Pittsburgh had dominated the Los Angeles Rams in Super Bowl XIV, providing a satisfying conclusion to the 1979 season, the Oakland Raiders, San Francisco 49ers, and Washington Redskins had climbed to the top in the three recent years.

NFL playoff history, following the 1979 campaign, had seen the Steelers fail to make the

Denver Broncos quarterback John Elway gets flushed out of the pocket by Steelers linebacker Mike Merriweather during the Broncos' 24–17 loss to the Pittsburgh Steelers in the 1984 AFC divisional playoff game. *Getty Images*

1980 and 1981 playoffs, redeeming in 1982 but losing the AFC first-round game: San Diego 31, Pittsburgh 28. It was quarterback Terry Bradshaw's 19th and final playoff appearance. He threw for 325 yards in the losing effort, giving up a deadly interception at the wire.

The following year, 1983, Bradshaw hung on but played in just one regular-season game—a shadow likeness of the Super Bowl XIV MVP. Even the Steelers' 1970s rivals in Oakland had just changed their address.

Yes, the Steelers would make the playoffs but would lose 38–10 to the Los Angeles Raiders in the 1983 AFC divisional postseason game.

# Game Details

## Pittsburgh 24 • Denver 17

**Location:** Mile High Stadium, Denver, Colorado

**Attendance:** 74,981

**Box Score:**

| Steelers | 0 | 10 | 7 | 7 | **24** |
|---|---|---|---|---|---|
| Broncos | 7 | 0 | 10 | 0 | **17** |

*Scoring:*
DEN Wright 9-yard pass from Elway (Karlis PAT)
PIT Anderson 28-yard FG
PIT Pollard 1-yard run (Anderson PAT)
DEN Karlis 21-yard FG
DEN Watson 20-yard pass from Elway (Karlis PAT)
PIT Lipps 10-yard pass from Malone (Anderson PAT)
PIT Pollard 2-yard run (Anderson PAT)

| Team | FD | RUSH | A-C-I | PASS |
|---|---|---|---|---|
| **Steelers** | 25 | 40/169 | 28-17-0 | 212 |
| **Broncos** | 15 | 22/51 | 38-20-2 | 199 |

# FOUR CHUCK NOLL MOMENTS BY THE DECADE

Pittsburgh Steelers head coach Chuck Noll got his first Three Rivers Stadium victory against the Buffalo Bills on October 11, 1970.

On January 6, 1980, the Steelers beat the Houston Oilers in the AFC Championship Game. Two weeks later Pittsburgh would dominate the Los Angeles Rams to win its fourth Super Bowl.

Noll picked up his 200th coaching victory against the New England Patriots on December 9, 1990.

Things were decidedly different. The 1983 season would also prove to be Franco Harris's last with Pittsburgh as well, and he would retire after his 1984 time with the Seattle Seahawks.

Steelers Nation needed something to carry it through during this transitional phase of Black and Gold history, and that brings us to the 1984 divisional playoff game at Denver's Mile High Stadium.

In truth, Pittsburgh head coach Chuck Noll still roamed the sideline, a stoic observer and enduring mastermind of the Steelers, seemingly indifferent to his team's dominant legacy or diminishing vitality, concentrating hard on the high-altitude game to be played.

Some history: back on September 4, 1983, in John Elway's rookie season and first NFL game—the first one against the Pittsburgh Steelers, for that matter—the Denver quarterback approached his offensive line. Problem was, he lined up behind his guard. He went on to complete one of eight pass attempts for 14 yards. Intercepted once, he was also sacked four times. He was pulled and replaced by Steve DeBerg, and the Broncos won 14–10.

Um, maybe Elway was a little intimidated.

But that was more than one year prior to this game, and this was a different situation, a playoff game when the stakes were high. The Broncos had rolled to a 13–3 record that 1984 regular season. Elway would now get his first NFL playoff start.

# FRANK POLLARD FACTS

In nostalgic sports-bar discussions about Steelers running backs, names like John Henry Johnson, Franco Harris, and Jerome Bettis naturally surface. So should Frank Pollard.

Picked in the 11th round of the 1980 NFL draft, the 5'10" and 218-pound Pollard came to Pittsburgh after playing his college ball at Baylor University.

During the 1981 season, he ranked ninth in the NFL with 4.6 yards per attempt.

In nine NFL seasons—all with the Steelers—he recorded the following statistics: 3,989 yards on 953 carries (4.2 yards per touch), and 20 touchdowns. He also caught 104 passes for 872 yards (8.4 yards per reception).

Name recognition, indeed.

For three quarters the teams exchanged leads. In the first quarter, Elway completed a nine-yard pass for a touchdown. With the score 7–0 in Denver's favor in the second, Pittsburgh got on the board with a 28-yard Gary Anderson field goal. The Steelers followed with a one-yard run by running back Frank Pollard. Pittsburgh led 10–7 at the half. This was feeling pretty good.

After the break, Denver started off with a third-quarter field goal, followed by Elway tossing another touchdown pass, this one for 20 yards. Here at home in Colorado, the future Hall of Fame inductee (2004 class) didn't look all that intimidated anymore.

Denver 17, Pittsburgh 10—the score said enough. But the Steelers weren't done just yet. Quarterback Mark Malone hit his man Louis Lipps, the rookie wideout, for 10 yards and a touchdown. Anderson's point after tied it up.

Fourth-quarter play—the mistake and turnover to follow—would decide it. With the game tied, 17–17, with three minutes to go, Elway dropped back. Maybe the nightmare of his first game against the Steelers the previous season came shuddering back into his mind. Maybe he just made a simple mistake—young quarterbacks, even those with future busts in Canton, might do that.

Whatever it was, defensive back Eric Williams—looking like Mel Blount, Mike Wagner, and the other Black and Gold coverage greats during the dynasty years—saw it coming. You could say that Elway telegraphed the throw, as Williams looked the pass in and claimed it.

Interception in hand, Williams had the end zone in mind and was stopped just short at the 2-yard line. Pollard took the ball in for the winning score, his second touchdown of the game. Anderson chipped in the extra point.

It was easily the sweetest Steelers victory that season, and the play that made it possible is one of the greatest ever, full of late-game thrills and franchise redemption.

# JOE GREENE LOCKS DOWN HOUSTON

The defensive tackle locked down the Houston Oilers in a one-man Steel Curtain performance that included five sacks, a blocked field goal, and a forced and recovered fumble

**T**he thing about defensive struggles in games such as this is that they often lack the flair of a deep pass or a long run. Still, defensive plays are the X factors that win big games.

Talk about fighting your way out of a hole, though. In some ways the Steelers were down for the count before they even started. Tackles Gerry Mullins and Jon Kolb had the flu bug. Defensive end L.C. Greenwood didn't play. Nor did guard Sam Davis.

During the game matters grew even worse. Quarterback Terry Bradshaw dislocated his finger. Guards Jim Clack (injured ankle) and Bruce Van Dyke (pulled calf muscle) left the game. If these casualties weren't enough, wide

They called him "Mean" Joe Greene for a reason. Here the Steelers defensive tackle watches from the sidelines in a November 1972 game. *Getty Images*

receiver Ron Shanklin and defensive end Craig Hanneman—the guy who replaced Greenwood—were also injured during the rugged contest and exited stage left. Some of the guys who got dinged up hung on, though—they had to. Defensive tackle Steve Furness and defensive end Dwight White, also hurt along the way, stayed on duty to stop the mounting Steelers sideline body count.

Who would step up?

The Steelers needed a stellar performance and a major defensive play to shut down the Houston Oilers. Joe Greene's performance clearly reflected a sense of urgency, even anger, at the mounting situation. He was ready, willing, and able to do the job of many men, to take the place of his fallen teammates. True enough, Houston was only 1–11 going into the game, but with all the Pittsburgh players down for the count, you could certainly argue the playing field—Astroturf, in this case—was evened up a little.

Forget that Houston only had one win going in. The Oilers could be spoilers.

Enter the Pittsburgh defensive line giant Greene, all 6′4″ and 275 pounds of him. First Greene sacked Houston quarterback Dan Pastorini, not just once, but twice, in the second quarter. "Going after the quarterback is like playing king of the mountain," Greene has said. "When you get the quarterback, you're on top of the mountain."

Greene then stifled a 25-yard field-goal try by kicker Skip Butler as the first half wound down. This, like a reliever coming out of the bullpen in a tight baseball game, kept the score tied 3–3. The second half would determine the win.

Ever-ready Steelers kicker Roy Gerela—often an important facet of the Pittsburgh dominance in the 1970s, and most certainly a crucial piece of the team's puzzle—put the Steeltown franchise ahead 6–3 in

That No. 75, he's going to be great. He's as strong as a bull and so blasted quick. I don't know how anyone's going to handle him in a year or two. Believe me, I don't know how you handle him now.

—Browns guard Gene Hickerson in 1969

the third quarter. Reliable kickers matter in such tough games. While Gerela certainly had some ups and downs during his career, his 39-yard field goal offered momentum. That's what set the stage for what would come next.

A place in the playoffs was still on the line.

The Steelers could still clinch their division—but not without somebody coming up big. The defensive play of the game represented this effort.

Why is No. 75's multiple-effort play so important?

With the Steelers leading just 6–3, and the Pittsburgh offense and defense riddled by injury and illness, Greene tore into the Houston backfield and in quick, methodical succession dumped running back

# Game Details

## Pittsburgh 9 • Houston 3

**Location:** Houston Astrodome, Houston, Texas

**Attendance:** 36,528

**Box Score:**

| | | | | | |
|---|---|---|---|---|---|
| **Steelers** | 3 | 0 | 6 | 0 | **9** |
| **Oilers** | 0 | 3 | 0 | 0 | **3** |

*Scoring:*
PIT Gerela 24-yard FG
HOU Butler 34-yard FG
PIT Gerela 39-yard FG
PIT Gerela 13-yard FG

| Team | FD | RUSH | A-C-I | PASS |
|---|---|---|---|---|
| **Steelers** | 12 | 38/130 | 19-10-0 | 63 |
| **Oilers** | 11 | 30/72 | 24-13-0 | 87 |

Fred Willis for a 12-yard loss, forced the ball out of his grasp, and somehow managed to recover it himself on the Oilers' 13-yard line. Greene's tackle of Willis, his crucial forced fumble, and the thrilling recovery on that single play all but sealed the deal.

Gerela's kick made it 9–3, which was all the Steelers needed.

By the game's end, Greene had stopped Houston's effort to get three more points with his blocked kick before halftime, and he made the two second-half Gerela field goals possible.

## PLAY AND PLAYER FACTS

Joe Greene's critical tackle, subsequent forced fumble, and recovery helped begin divisional title wins that would total seven in the 1970s.

Greene earned his position as one of the greatest defensive tackles of all time with his effort against Houston on December 10, 1972. Still, it's hard for devoted fans to believe that the Pittsburgh Post-Gazette once ran the provocative headline, "Who's Joe Greene?" the day following the NFL draft that brought the North Texas State University player to the Steelers. He had come to the team in 1969 as new head coach Chuck Noll's number-one draft pick.

Both Noll and Greene joined a team that had turned only eight winning seasons in the 36 years since the franchise entered the NFL in 1933.

Known for his famous No. 75, Greene briefly wore No. 72 during his rookie season. Greene's No. 75 and Ernie Stautner's No. 70 are the only two numbers Pittsburgh has officially retired.

When all was said and done, Greene—named NFL Defensive Player of the Year in 1972 and 1974—had contributed much to six conference championship games and four Super Bowl rings.

"Joe Who?" Joe Greene—an unknown draft pick who finished with 10 Pro Bowls to his credit.

Two weeks later, on December 23, Pittsburgh would beat the Oakland Raiders in the 1972 AFC divisional playoff game for the first playoff win in Steelers history. It wouldn't have been possible without Greene's single-handed effort—this crucial tackle, forced fumble, and recovery.

And that's why team captain Andy Russell awarded the game ball to Greene and why his monumental defensive effort—especially his multiple-statistic play—is so important. It was clearly the beginning of the best years to come.

Reminiscing about this play, a fan can see instant connections with James Harrison's 2007 multistatistical performance against the Ravens on Monday Night Football and dramatic tackle on a punt return, with Greene himself looking on.

# SPECIAL CONSIDERATION

# ANDERSON DRILLS 50-YARD GAME WINNER

Pittsburgh Steelers kicker Gary Anderson drills a 50-yard field goal in overtime for a dramatic playoff win

**I**t was one of those NFL games you just knew would somehow end up tied at the end of regulation.

The Houston Oilers had beaten the Steelers twice during the regular season, but this was the playoffs, when anything can happen, even for an underdog like Pittsburgh (at least this particular year). Especially if a kicker like Gary Anderson is involved.

Born in Parys, South Africa, in 1959, Anderson moved to the United States with his family and later attended Syracuse University. Taken by the Buffalo Bills in the seventh round of the 1982 NFL draft, Anderson signed as a free agent with the Steelers after the Bills cut him before the regular season began. History-minded fans wonder how Buffalo would have fared with Anderson kicking instead of the Bills' Scott Norwood, whose potential game-winning 47-yard field goal went wide right with four seconds left in Super Bowl XXV.

Days after the Steelers signed Anderson, he and Pittsburgh faced the Dallas Cowboys. That Monday Night Football game introduced the rookie kicker to the NFL viewing audience as he went three for three in

# Game Details

## Pittsburgh 26 • Houston 23 (OT)

**Location:** Houston Astrodome, Houston, Texas

**Attendance:** 59,406

**Box Score:**

| Steelers | 7 | 3 | 3 | 10 | 3 | **26** |
|---|---|---|---|---|---|---|
| Oilers | 0 | 6 | 3 | 14 | 0 | **23** |

*Scoring:*
PIT Worley 9-yard run (Anderson PAT)
HOU Zendejas 26-yard FG
HOU Zendejas 35-yard FG
PIT Anderson 25-yard FG
HOU Zendejas 26-yard FG
PIT Anderson 30-yard FG
PIT Anderson 48-yard FG
HOU Givins 18-yard pass from Moon (Zendejas PAT)
HOU Givins 9-yard pass from Moon (Zendejas PAT)
PIT Hoge 2-yard run (Anderson PAT)
PIT Anderson 50-yard FG

| Team | FD | RUSH | A-C-I | PASS |
|---|---|---|---|---|
| Steelers | 17 | 30/177 | 33-15-0 | 112 |
| Oilers | 22 | 25/65 | 48-29-0 | 315 |

Gary Anderson holds many Steelers records: longest field goal (55 yards), field-goal attempts (395), field goals (309), and career team points (1,343). Here Anderson drills a field goal during the 1989 NFL season. *Getty Images*

field-goal tries, all of them in the second half as the Steelers won 36–28. Years later he'd still prove reliable, and that brings us to this memorable wild-card playoff game.

Chuck Noll hadn't won a playoff game in five years, and Pittsburgh fans, like their team's coach, needed one badly.

## OTHER ANDERSON CAREER HIGHLIGHTS

In his first season, cut by Buffalo and picked up by Pittsburgh, Anderson made the NFL's All-Rookie Team.

Gary Anderson—three men have played by that name in the NFL, by the way—kicked for the Pittsburgh Steelers (1982–1994), Philadelphia Eagles (1995–1996), San Francisco 49ers (1997), Minnesota Vikings (1998–2002), and Tennessee Titans (2003–2004) during his long career.

No stranger to game-winning kicks, on November 3, 1985, at Three Rivers Stadium, Anderson made a 25-yarder with nine seconds left to put the Steelers ahead 10–9 over their rival the Cleveland Browns. At the time, it was Pittsburgh's 16th-straight win over the Browns at home.

Anderson holds many Steelers records: longest field goal (55 yards), field-goal attempts (395), field goals (309), and career team points (1,343).

In 1998, in his post-Steelers days with the Minnesota Vikings, Anderson became the first NFL kicker to successfully make every field goal and point-after attempt during season play for a perfect regular season. The Colts' Mike Vanderjagt also did it, and his perfect run included the playoffs, as well.

Anderson ranks second on the all-time list for NFL points scored with 2,434. He also holds the NFL record for single-season points scored without touchdowns. In that 1998 season, he kicked 35 field goals and 59 point-after attempts for 164 total points.

A throwback of sorts, Anderson wore the one-bar facemask throughout his career.

The Steelers led 7–0 at the end of the first quarter on a nine-yard run by rookie running back Tim Worley. Anderson nailed the point after.

Next Anderson booted a 25-yard field goal in the second quarter, which ended with Pittsburgh leading 10–6 (two Houston field goals had put the Oilers on the board).

## ANOTHER KICKER, ANOTHER TIME

Lightning delayed the game for half an hour. Heavy rain made the grass field mush, even boglike, more like Heinz Swamp. Players slipped and slid, dropped passes, and lost their footing. It looked more like rugby, from which modern football had its origins, than the NFL.

The Monday Night Football game on November 26, 2007, stayed scoreless through one quarter, then two, then three, and into the fourth. That's when the Steelers and Ben Roethlisberger put on a sweet little play drive, with the ultimate goal of setting up Jeff Reed for the winning 24-yard field goal try.

Punter Daniel Sepulveda held it for Pittsburgh kicker Reed, and with 17 seconds to go on the Heinz Field clock, the wobbling, wet pigskin sailed through the uprights.

Steelers 3, Dolphins 0.

It was the first time in 64 years that an NFL game had stayed scoreless so long. It was the lowest-scoring Monday Night Football game since the show had first aired in 1970.

Wind. Rain. Gloom of night. Kickers matter. Somewhere Gary Anderson was smiling.

Following the 2007 NFL season, the Steelers officially affirmed that they would continue using grass at Heinz Field and would not install artificial turf, saying that Pittsburgh players preferred it because the natural surface reduces serious injuries.

And in this case, it lowered the score.

After halftime it remained an NFL kicker's game, as the Oilers' Tony Zendejas hit one more in the third, and Anderson put a 30-yard try through the uprights.

The Steelers' kicker would follow with a 48-yarder in the fourth quarter, but Houston wide receiver Ernest Givins and quarterback Warren Moon weren't done just yet. Not even close. In the fourth quarter the Oilers duo put two touchdowns on the board, and Zendejas hit both point-after attempts to make it Houston 23, Steelers 16.

But Pittsburgh wasn't done either, as running back Merril Hoge executed a crucial two-yard run to bring the Steelers within one point of tying. An important factor in Anderson's scoring this day, Hoge doggedly amassed 100 yards in the game. Anderson's point after tied the score and sent the contest into overtime.

Sudden-death situations sharpen football fans' minds into a double-edged emotional state: hope and dread. You have faith your team is surely the one destined to deliver that win. A loss is unimaginable at the time. But loss, that bitter pill, is part of the fan's experience.

In overtime Pittsburgh got into position to try that first option out. If they failed, the Oilers would have the ball with good field position. Make it, and...

With 59,406 Astrodome attendees looking on, Anderson settled in and calmly kicked the 50-yard game winner to put the Steelers into the 1989 AFC divisional playoff, where they'd ultimately lose 24–23—one of John Elway's classic comebacks. As a footnote, the January 7, 1990, game at Mile High Stadium would be Coach Noll's final postseason appearance.

Still, Anderson's game-winning wild-card field goal was nothing less than satisfying.

# PITTSBURGH'S ONSIDE KICK, RECOVERY, AND TOUCHDOWN

An unexpected onside kick with 11:20 left in Super Bowl XXX almost helps achieve a comeback win against the favored Cowboys

It was the fifth Steelers Super Bowl appearance, the third occasion they met the Cowboys in the big game, and the first time they didn't beat them in three chances.

There are a couple reasons why Dallas Cowboys cornerback Larry Brown held the Pete Rozelle Trophy for his MVP effort. But let's back up a bit. Let's look at the playoff run that put the Steelers in Sun Devil Stadium.

In the 1995 AFC divisional playoff game held at Three Rivers Stadium, Pittsburgh beat the Buffalo Bills on the strength of kicker Norm Johnson's reliable leg and Bam Morris's 106 running yards. After a comeback threat, Morris's two big touchdown runs boosted the score to 40–21 for a Steelers victory. Big win? It was the Bills' first playoff loss in 10 AFC games going back to the 1990 season.

Pittsburgh's cornerback and special teams player Deon Figures recovered Norm Johnson's onside kick and kept the Steelers in the game. For a moment, a Super Bowl XXX comeback seemed possible. *Getty Images*

Fast-forward to the 1995 AFC championship the following weekend. In this one, the Steelers held on to the wire and eluded yet another even stronger comeback bid by the opposition, this one by Indianapolis Colts quarterback Jim Harbaugh: Pittsburgh 20, Indianapolis 16. These two wins took the Steelers to Arizona for the big one.

It didn't take long before Dallas' dominance asserted itself by scoring on the first three possessions, putting the Cowboys up 13–zip. Nevertheless, Steelers quarterback Neil O'Donnell hit Yancey Thigpen for a six-yard touchdown pass just 13 seconds before halftime. Pittsburgh had pulled to within six points as Steelers Nation shifted its collective attitude from despair to hope.

O'Donnell—along with quarterbacks Mike Tomczak, a veteran, and rookies Jim Miller and Kordell Stewart—had led Pittsburgh to an 11–5 regular season. During the 1995 NFL campaign, O'Donnell had put up some decent numbers, specifically 246 completions on 416 attempts for 2,970 yards, 17 touchdowns, and just seven interceptions.

In the middle of the third quarter the Steelers had the ball at midfield, and things were looking good for the Black and Gold. How that can change in an NFL second! Suddenly Cowboys cornerback Brown intercepted O'Donnell and returned the pick 44 yards. Bang, bang—Dallas quarterback Troy Aikman hit Michael Irvin for 17, capitalizing on the turnover. Emmitt Smith then ran a yard for the score. Dallas went up 13 again.

Some of you groaned. Some of you cussed. Some of you optimists knew the game wasn't done just yet. And you were right.

Dallas had gone up by 13 points at the game's start. The Steelers had fought back with a score just before the half, doing it with 13 seconds to go. The Cowboys were now up again by 13. What's with that number, anyway? Steelers Nation bad-luck numerologists began to worry about the game's outcome again.

Ever-reliable Steelers kicker Johnson booted a 46-yard field goal early in the fourth quarter. That pulled Pittsburgh even closer, or at least stalled the Cowboys. Something had to be done—a big play, an unexpected move.

Onside kick, anyone?

Johnson intentionally booted the ball to the right sideline and short—but far enough so that it was up for grabs. Such a risky effort can either reward or punish the executioner. At best, the onside kick is intended to maximize the kicking team's chances of recovering the ball. At worst, it sacrifices good field position, offering it up to the opposition.

The Wilson football's regulation "prolate spheroid" shape, as defined by the NFL rulebook, makes either outcome possible.

Pittsburgh's Deon Figures recovered the desperate but calculated maneuver. O'Donnell, now in control of the ball, hit wide receiver Andre Hastings twice. O'Donnell delivered to wideout Ernie Mills next. And with 6:36 left to play, Morris ran it home for a score. The Steelers were now within three points of tying it up.

Bold move. Big turnaround.

# Game Details

## Dallas 27 • Pittsburgh 17

**Location:** Sun Devil Stadium, Phoenix, Arizona

**Attendance:** 76,347

**Box Score:**

| | | | | | |
|---|---|---|---|---|---|
| **Cowboys** | 10 | 3 | 7 | 7 | **27** |
| **Steelers** | 0 | 7 | 0 | 10 | **17** |

*Scoring:*
DAL Boniol 42-yard FG
DAL Novacek 3-yard pass from Aikman (Boniol PAT)
DAL Boniol 35-yard FG
PIT Thigpen 6-yard pass from O'Donnell (N. Johnson PAT)
DAL E. Smith 1-yard run (Boniol PAT)
PIT N. Johnson 46-yard FG
PIT Morris 1-yard run (N. Johnson PAT)
DAL E. Smith 4-yard run (Boniol PAT)

| Team | FD | RUSH | A-C-I | PASS |
|---|---|---|---|---|
| **Cowboys** | 15 | 25/56 | 23-15-0 | 198 |
| **Steelers** | 25 | 31/103 | 49-28-3 | 207 |

Neil O'Donnell (shown getting sacked by Chad Hennings in the second quarter) threw three second-half interceptions that helped undermine the Steelers' Super Bowl comeback against the Cowboys. *AP Images*

Next, Pittsburgh took possession on its 32-yard line after a forced Cowboys punt. But Brown was still on the field, and he was in that big-play zone that certain defensive backs achieve in such games. As if destined to control the ultimate outcome, the Super Bowl XXX MVP intercepted O'Donnell again, stealing the ball out of the air at the 39-yard line and returning it 33 yards to the 6. Not long after, Smith ran for the clinching score.

Want more fan pain? O'Donnell would throw yet one more symbolic interception on the last play of the game, this one pulled in by Brock Marion. These three turnovers were the only ones during Super Bowl XXX.

Yes, Dallas was favored by 13½ going into the game, but take away those two Brown interceptions that set up two Cowboys touchdowns and the Steelers would likely have won it. Statistically, Pittsburgh outgained Dallas 310 to 254 in total yardage. The defense held the Cowboys to just 56 running yards. The Black and Gold also racked up 25 first downs to Dallas's 15.

It felt like it could have happened.

Instead, the Dallas Cowboys won their third ring in four years. They also tied the San Francisco 49ers for the most Super Bowl team victories at the time: five.

It was Pittsburgh's first Super Bowl loss in team history, and it hurt.

# NORM JOHNSON'S 45-YARD FIELD GOAL

In a playoff win over the Bills, Norm Johnson's long field goal would be the highlight of a day when he put 16 points on the board himself

**H**ere's another Steelers trivia question for that downtime at your local sports bar. Who ranks seventh on the all-time NFL scoring list? Norm Johnson, that's who.

As of this writing, Johnson's 1,736 points over 18 seasons establish him in that spot. When you put on an NFL uniform for almost two decades, it surely speaks for something—reliability.

Kicker Johnson proved worthy with four teams: the Seattle Seahawks (1982–1990), Atlanta Falcons (1991–1994), Pittsburgh Steelers (1995–1998), and Philadelphia Eagles (1999). His longevity ensured that his four seasons with the Black and Gold would include many memorable games during the Bill Cowher era, when wins were helped or claimed as a result of Johnson's leg.

Steelers kicker Norm Johnson contributed 16 points in the 40–21 AFC divisional playoff win over the Bills. Johnson is shown making one of his field-goal attempts during the contest. *Getty Images*

# KICKING: A BRIEF HISTORY

**1904:** Points for field goals set at four, down from the original five in the early days of professional football.

**1909:** Field goal points change to three.

**1932:** Goal posts move from end lines to goal lines.

**1946:** Forward passes ruled incomplete on hitting goal posts.

**1948:** A flexible artificial kickoff tee now permitted.

**1960:** American Football League adds two-point option for points after a touchdown.

**1966:** Yellow goal posts now offset from goal line. Uprights 20 feet above the crossbar standardized.

**1967:** So-called slingshot goal posts become an NFL standard.

**1970:** After the 26-team NFL merger, the point after is ruled one point.

**1974:** Goal posts move back from the goal line to the end lines. Missed field goals from beyond the 20-yard line now see the football returned to the line of scrimmage.

**1994:** A two-point conversion option is added. Following a touchdown, NFL teams can now run or pass for two points or kick a point after for one. (College football has used the two-point conversion since 1958, as did the AFL between 1960–1969. Adoption was delayed even after the 1970 NFL-AFL league merger.)

**2000:** Celebrations limited to a single on-field player—this includes kickers. On October 22, 2000, Gary Anderson, playing for the Minnesota Vikings, made a 21-yard field goal against the Buffalo Bills to pass George Blanda as the all-time NFL scoring leader (2,004 points at the time). He was not penalized for celebrating. (Note: Kicker Morten Andersen—no relation and a different spelling—now leads all-time NFL scorers with 2,544 points. Anderson holds steady in second place.)

**2005:** During field-goal or extra-point attempts, the defensive team is now penalized for unsportsmanlike conduct if they attempt consecutive timeouts to distract or "ice" the kicker.

**2006:** Defenders can no longer line up over the long snapper during field-goal or extra-point attempts.

Fans and observers didn't call him "Mr. Automatic" for nothing. They sometimes referred to former Steelers kicker Gary Anderson by that nickname for the same reason.

A West Coast guy, Johnson was born in Inglewood, California, on May 31, 1960. He attended UCLA, graduated with a bachelor's degree in economics, and later would become a real estate agent after his playing days concluded. As with many competent NFL kickers, he became something of a journeyman despite his effectiveness.

That brought him to the Steelers in 1995, a season when he'd have his best year. In '95, Johnson led the NFL in field goals made: 34 of 41. He nailed all of his extra point attempts as well: 39 of them. Then in this highlighted Saturday playoff game against the Bills, he claimed four field goals. In the AFC title game against the Colts the following Sunday, he'd kick two. In the Steelers' Super Bowl XXX loss, he'd nail a 46-yard try.

Don't blame any Pittsburgh defeats on Johnson that season.

As for the big 1995 AFC divisional playoff win over the Buffalo Bills, it was defense, some running, a little passing, and Johnson's leg that shored up the victory. Consider his single-game effort. Pittsburgh struck first on a one-yard John L. Williams run. Johnson kicked the point after. Ernie Mills caught a 10-yard pass from Neil O'Donnell. Johnson made the extra point. Johnson then kicked the 45-yard field goal, then another for 38 to put the Steelers up 20–zip.

# Game Details

## Pittsburgh 40 • Buffalo 21

**Location:** Three Rivers Stadium, Pittsburgh, Pennsylvania

**Attendance:** 59,072

**Box Score:**

| | | | | | |
|---|---|---|---|---|---|
| **Bills** | 0 | 7 | 7 | 7 | **21** |
| **Steelers** | 7 | 16 | 3 | 14 | **40** |

*Scoring:*

PIT J.L. Williams 1-yard run (N. Johnson PAT)
PIT Mills 10-yard pass from O'Donnell (N. Johnson PAT)
PIT N. Johnson 45-yard FG
PIT N. Johnson 38-yard FG
BUF Thomas 1-yard run (Christie PAT)
PIT N. Johnson 34-yard FG
PIT N. Johnson 39-yard FG
BUF Cline 2-yard pass from Van Pelt (Christie PAT)
BUF Thomas 9-yard pass from Kelly (Christie PAT)
PIT Morris 13-yard run (N. Johnson PAT)
PIT Morris 2-yard run (N. Johnson PAT)

| Team | FD | RUSH | A-C-I | PASS |
|---|---|---|---|---|
| **Bills** | 18 | 21/94 | 39–18–3 | 156 |
| **Steelers** | 23 | 43/147 | 35–19–2 | 262 |

Buffalo got on the board with a one-yard Thurman Thomas run and follow-up point after, but Johnson countered with another field goal, this one for 34 yards. If this wasn't enough, he followed with another, reaching 39.

The next two scores, both touchdowns, would involve the Bills staging a comeback on passes from Alex Van Pelt, the reserve Buffalo quarterback, and Jim Kelly, the starter who showed some wear and tear during this game. Bam Morris's 13-yard run for Pittsburgh and Johnson's point after put a stop to that bleeding.

Morris's two-yard run and Johnson's last points of the game, the extra one, clinched the big win.

Total game points generated by Johnson's leg: 16.

Johnson's NFL career stats include 477 field-goal tries, with 366 made for a 76.7 percentage. He hit 638 points after touchdowns. Though his two Pro-Bowl nominations and All-Pro selections came outside his Steelers playing days (1984, 1993), he'll always be remembered for some clutch kicks and steady contributions wearing the black-and-gold No. 9 uniform.

*Postscript: Matt Bahr, another Black and Gold kicker, eventually led his team to a Super Bowl XIV victory against the Los Angeles Rams in his rookie Steelers season (1979). He contributed seven total game points on a field goal and four points after in that win.*

*Along with former Steelers kickers Anderson (2,434 career points) and Johnson (1,736), Bahr ranks 25th among the top 30 leading lifetime scorers in NFL history (1,422 points). Anderson remains the second all-time NFL scorer.*

*Yet another journeyman kicker, Bahr played his first two seasons with Pittsburgh, moved on to the San Francisco 49ers (1981), Cleveland Browns (1981–1989), New York Giants (1990–1992), Philadelphia Eagles (1993), and New England Patriots (1993–1995). Over 17 seasons he amassed 300 field goals (on 415 tries) and 522 extra points (on 534 efforts). His older brother Chris Bahr also spent 14 years as an NFL kicker (1976–1989).*

# REGGIE HARRISON'S BLOCKED PUNT

In Super Bowl X's fourth quarter, Pittsburgh's Reggie Harrison blocked Mitch Hoopes's punt—with his face

**R**eggie Harrison had never blocked a punt before. Not in high school. Not at the University of Cincinnati. Not in the NFL.

"I was always afraid to block a kick before, for fear of being kicked myself," Harrison has said.

Reserve running back Harrison was a relatively unknown 5'11" and 218-pound footballer selected in the ninth round of the 1974 NFL draft. He played in one game for the St. Louis (football) Cardinals before coming to Pittsburgh in 1974, where he took the field for four more games that season.

Fast forward to Super Bowl X, the culmination of the 1975 campaign.

Dallas led 10–7 in the fourth quarter. Punter Mitch Hoopes inherited the task of booting the ball from their 16-yard line. It was one of those moments that could go either way. A decent punt would put the Steelers at midfield or close to it,

Dallas Cowboys punter Mitch Hoopes, pictured here, booted one ball into Reggie Harrison's face during Super Bowl X. This put two safety points on the board as the pigskin rolled out of the end zone. That's Steelers linebacker Jack Lambert, No. 58, rushing Hoopes. *Getty Images*

and they might put on a drive. The Cowboys could also hold them there and regain possession.

Then again, why bother to go through all of that when you can block the punt?

As Cowboys coach Tom Landry later said dismissively, "They [the Steelers] rushed 10 men, and somebody missed a block. I don't know who it was. We probably just brush-blocked Harrison, and he made the big play. That's usually what happens on a blocked punt."

And that's pretty much what did happen. In short, Harrison blocked the punt, taking it in his face, splitting his tongue on impact. His fears

The Pittsburgh Steelers huddle around quarterback Terry Bradshaw, No. 12, during Super Bowl X against the Dallas Cowboys. *Getty Images*

Hollywood was on hand at Super Bowl X to shoot suspense sequences for the 1977 film Black Sunday. Based on the Thomas Harris novel, the R-rated action thriller stars Bruce Dern as the character Lander, who pilots the Goodyear blimp over the Orange Bowl with evil intent. Even Terry Bradshaw and Roger Staubach make appearances. Miami Dolphins owner Joe Robbie played himself, and when confronted with the terrorist threat on American soil—now eerily prophetic after 9/11, some might say—Robbie utters the words: "Cancel the Super Bowl? That's like canceling Christmas!"

were surely confirmed, but for the betterment of the team. The ball rolled right out of the end zone for the score—a safety.

Weird points, but they counted.

You'll remember Dwight White's safety from Super Bowl IX the year before. Here we had another important safety the second year in a row. Score: Dallas 10, Pittsburgh 9.

As the Official Rules of the NFL states, "After a safety, the team scored upon must next put the ball in play by a free kick (punt, dropkick, or placekick)." As a result, following the big Harrison play, the Steelers gained possession.

Fated, it seemed. Pittsburgh proceeded to put on a drive. This concluded on fourth down at the Cowboys' 20-yard line, where kicker Roy Gerela kicked a 36-yard field goal.

The five-point momentum shift following Harrison's special-teams play meant everything: Steelers 12, Cowboys 10.

On the next drive, Pittsburgh safety Mike Wagner intercepted Cowboys quarterback Roger Staubach and took the ball to the 7-yard line. Gerela's 18-yard field goal soon upped the score to 15–10, with Steelers in the lead—and they never let up.

If Harrison's blocked punt is the turning point Pittsburgh fans remember, it's Wagner's stellar defensive plays following it that shored up the game. Not only did he intercept Staubach to set up Gerela's second field goal of the day, but on the game's last play—a Hail Mary pass—the don't-quit-until-the-gun-sounds Wagner deflected the ball to Steelers teammate Glen Edwards, who returned the interception upfield to claim victory.

Steelers fans certainly remember that this Super Bowl showcased Lynn Swann's ball-catching skills as well, and that he overcame adversity going into the game, combating the lingering effects of a concussion from the week before.

# Game Details

## Pittsburgh 21 • Dallas 17

**Location:** Orange Bowl, Miami, Florida

**Attendance:** 80,187

**Box Score:**

| | | | | | |
|---|---|---|---|---|---|
| **Steelers** | 7 | 0 | 0 | 14 | **21** |
| **Cowboys** | 7 | 3 | 0 | 7 | **17** |

*Scoring:*

DAL D. Pearson 29-yard pass from Staubach (Fritsch PAT)

PIT Grossman 7-yard pass from Bradshaw (Gerela PAT)

DAL Fritsch 36-yard FG

PIT Harrison blocked Hoopes's punt through end zone for safety

PIT Gerela 36-yard FG

PIT Gerela 18-yard FG

PIT Swann 64-yard pass from Bradshaw (PAT failed)

DAL P. Howard 34-yard pass from Staubach (Fritsch PAT)

| Team | FD | RUSH | A-C-I | PASS |
|---|---|---|---|---|
| **Steelers** | 13 | 46/149 | 19-9-0 | 190 |
| **Cowboys** | 14 | 31/108 | 24-15-3 | 162 |

Harrison's blocked punt remains a career play for the Somerville, New Jersey, native and reserve running back who rushed 139 times for 631 yards and 4.5 yards per carry in his four seasons with the Steelers. He posted eight touchdowns and seven receptions for 36 yards along the way as well.

As for punter Hoopes, 1975 would be his only season with Dallas, and one of his three in the NFL. He split the 1976 season between the San Diego Chargers and Houston Oilers and spent 1977 with the Detroit Lions. As a career punter, he booted 123 for 4,760 yards—his longest went 57 yards.

Four career Hoopes punts were blocked—five including Harrison's Super Bowl postseason play.

# THE WAGNER FACTOR

A Steelers 11th-round selection out of Western Illinois University in the 1971 NFL draft, defensive back Mike Wagner played his entire career with Pittsburgh (1971–1980). The 6'1" and 210-pound safety started as a Steelers rookie and never looked back.

In 1973 he led the NFL in interceptions with eight and hauled in 36 over his 10-year career for a total of 491 return yards. He also recovered 12 fumbles for 93 yards.

A two-time Pro Bowl player—1976 and 1977, not the year he led the NFL in pass picks, you'll note—Wagner was a better-than-average defensive back who brought poise, quiet leadership, and demonstrative pass-stealing ability to the game, an essential piece of the Steel Curtain defense.

Along the way he played in four Super Bowls, all wins.

# JEFF REED'S OVERTIME FIELD GOAL

In an AFC divisional playoff game Jets kicker Doug Brien misses two key kicks, but Pittsburgh's kicker connects for a 20-17 win

**N**FL kickers don't get much respect. Maybe it's because they don't usually make big hits—unless it's nailing a crucial field goal, that is.

True enough, there's only one NFL kicker enshrined in the Hall of Fame: Jan Stenerud. Others certainly should be there, including kicker Gary Anderson (5'11" and 193 pounds), who played 13 of his 23 seasons with the Pittsburgh Steelers. Maybe it's because kickers are such specialists. And often big of leg but slight of body—unless you're Morten Andersen (different spelling and 6'2" and 217 pounds), a durable kicker whose statistics over 25 years will earn him a Canton statue someday.

We certainly notice these guys when they kick game winners. We also notice them when they miss.

There was a lot on the line on January 15, 2005, namely the postseason win.

Pittsburgh Steelers kicker Jeff Reed celebrates with punter and holder Chris Gardocki after kicking the winning overtime field goal against the New York Jets in the 2004 AFC divisional playoff game at Heinz Field. *Getty Images*

As an aside, Steelers quarterback Ben Roethlisberger's rookie-season winning streak was also still intact. If you were a Steelers (or Jets) fan watching the game, an observer would have seen you scream and yell with both joy and worry.

In the end, two kickers would decide the game.

Let's back up a bit. A quick look at the game's box score during regulation play would reveal the numbers 10 and seven, alternately shared by both teams. Pittsburgh put up 10 points in the first quarter, zero in the second and third quarters, and seven points in the fourth. After seeing the Steelers go up 10–0 in the first quarter, the Jets would score 10 in the second. They also scored seven in the third, owning the middle of the game. In the fourth quarter, New York could do nothing. Zero.

By the end of regulation the game ended where it started: tied.

Along the way it was fits and starts, poor play and perfect execution by both teams—a clinic in the highs and lows of NFL fandom. Along the way Jerome Bettis would also run for 101 yards. Hines Ward would earn 105 more on pass receptions. That's some of the good. But again, in the end, it was a kicker's game.

With the score tied 17–17, the game clock taunting fate with 1:58 left in the fourth quarter, the Jets' Doug Brien had a shot at winning the game. The kick would have to reach out there: 47 yards, in fact. The thing is, Brien's field-goal try nearly had the distance and accuracy—the two basics for this kind of heroic play—until it hit the goal post, that is.

So what did the Steelers and their rookie quarterback do right after that Jets field-goal miss? They offered the football back to New York for another try, as defensive back David Barrett intercepted Big Ben like he was designated to catch the belated gift (Barrett's birthday fell just weeks before).

Could it get any worse?

The Jets put on another drive, slowly, surely, and moved the ball to the 24-yard line. It was plain to see what they wanted to do. They wanted to offer their kicker a chance at redemption. Brien would have another shot at glory.

# Game Details

## Pittsburgh 20 • New York Jets 17 (OT)

**Location:** Heinz Field, Pittsburgh, Pennsylvania

**Attendance:** 64,915

**Box Score:**

| | | | | | | |
|---|---|---|---|---|---|---|
| **Jets** | 0 | 10 | 7 | 0 | 0 | **17** |
| **Steelers** | 10 | 0 | 0 | 7 | 3 | **20** |

*Scoring:*

PIT Reed 45-yard FG
PIT Bettis 3-yard run (Reed PAT)
NYJ Brien 42-yard FG
NYJ Moss 75-yard punt return (Brien PAT)
NYJ Tongue 86-yard interception return (Brien PAT)
PIT Ward 4-yard pass from Roethlisberger (Reed PAT)
PIT Reed 33-yard FG

| Team | FD | RUSH | A-C-I | PASS |
|---|---|---|---|---|
| Jets | 17 | 27/110 | 33-21-1 | 165 |
| Steelers | 23 | 43/193 | 30-17-2 | 171 |

> I'm not going to say it was a miracle…. But that's the closest thing to it I've ever seen.
>
> **—Steelers linebacker Larry Foote**

# JEFF REED FACTS

Kicker Jeff Reed played for the Steelers for all but five games of his entire NFL career, nine seasons all told (2002–2010).

Born in Kansas City, Missouri, the 5'11" and 226-pound Reed was an undrafted free agent in 2002. He'd played his college ball at the University of North Carolina at Chapel Hill, where he'd been a journalism major.

Prior to college, Reed attended East Mecklenburg High School in Charlotte, North Carolina, where he kicked for the football team, nailing a 54-yard field goal his senior year. He also captained the soccer team, lettering in both sports.

Reed's honors include second-team All-ACC as a college junior and honorable mention All-ACC team as a senior. His 66 consecutive extra points set a UNC record. The future Steelers footballer would also be among those players nominated for the Lou Groza Award, given to the nation's top college place-kicker.

"Guaranteed" Reed has kicked a number of memorable game-winning field goals: 2005's clutch kick against the Jets, a 2005 regular-season, 40-yard field goal against the San Diego Chargers on Monday Night Football to win it 24–22 with six seconds left, and a Halloween kick of 37 yards to beat the Baltimore Ravens 20–19, also in 2005. He also kicked game-winners in 2008 and 2009 against the Ravens and Titans, respectively.

It's safe to say the Steelers Super Bowl XL appearance would not have been possible without him.

Reed made the only points either team scored in the Monday Night Football mud fest on November 26, 2007, a game winner of 24 yards with 17 seconds to go on the Heinz Field clock: Steelers 3, Dolphins 0.

Kickers. They matter.

Yes, Brien, the same kicker who made the winning overtime field goal against the San Diego Chargers the previous week. That AFC wild-card game field goal of 28 yards made the final score 20–17—the outcome of this one, too, if the Jets kicker could put it through the uprights.

Back in the distant second quarter, Brien had made a 42-yarder for the Jets' first score. He could surely do it again for the game winner at one yard more, right?

Steelers fans stared wide-eyed into the car wreck that was about to happen.

The snap, the set, the kick, and the ball sailed...wide. It wasn't even close. On the Pittsburgh sideline, in the Heinz Field stands, and likely in your television room or local sports bar if you're a Steelers fan reading this, it looked more like a live concert's mosh pit than in-your-seat entertainment.

Disaster was averted. But the score was still tied.

Overtime play began, exerting its slow torture on the minds of Jets fans who realized they could have won the game in regulation—twice.

So with more than 12 minutes of the fifth quarter gone, the Steelers' kicker, Jeff Reed, stepped up to kick the field goal. His 33-yarder strong-legged the Jets into submission.

It was as simple as that.

In the process the Jets became the first NFL team to play three consecutive overtime games (a regular-season loss to the St. Louis Rams had preceded their wild-card win over San Diego).

Reed had put the first points of the game on the board way back in the first quarter (a 45-yard field goal) and the last of the day, the game winner.

He earned that hard-won kicker's respect in this one.

# SELECTED BIBLIOGRAPHY

*America's Game: The Super Bowl Champions: Pittsburgh Steelers Collection.* DVD. NFL Productions LLC, 2007.

Bettis, Jerome, with Teresa Varley. *Driving Home: My Unforgettable Super Bowl Run.* Chicago: Triumph Books, 2006.

Blount, Roy, Jr.. *About Three Bricks Shy...and the Load Filled Up.* Pittsburgh: University of Pittsburgh Press, 2004.

Chastain, Bill. *Steel Dynasty: The Team That Changed the NFL.* Chicago: Triumph Books, 2005.

Mendelson, Abby. *The Pittsburgh Steelers: The Official Team History.* 3rd edition. Lanham, MD: Taylor Trade Publishing, 2006.

National Football League. *Official Rules of the NFL.* Chicago: Triumph Books, 2007.

National Football League. "Official Site of the National Football League," http://www.nfl.com/

Palmer, Pete (ed.), et al. *The ESPN Pro Football Encyclopedia.* 2nd edition. New York: Sterling Publishing Co., 2007.

Paolantonio, Sal, with Reuben Frank. *The Paolantonio Report.* Chicago: Triumph Books, 2007.

*Pittsburgh Post-Gazette. Cowher Power: 14 Years of Tradition with the Pittsburgh Steelers.* Chicago: Triumph Books, 2006.

*Pittsburgh Post-Gazette. Decade of Power: The Pittsburgh Steelers in the Cowher Era,* Chicago: Triumph Books, 2002.

*Pittsburgh Post-Gazette.* Post-Gazette NOW, Steelers/NFL, http://www.post-gazette.com/steelers/

Pro Football Hall of Fame. "Official Site of the Pro Football Hall of Fame," http://www.profootballhof.com/.

Professional Football Researchers Association, http://www.profootballresearch.com/.

Rooney, Dan, David F. Halaas, and Andrew E. Masich. *Dan Rooney: My 75 Years with the Pittsburgh Steelers and the NFL.* New York: Da Capo Press, 2007.

*Steelers: Road to XL.* DVD. NFL Productions LLC, 2006.

*Steelers: The Complete History.* DVD. NFL Productions LLC, 2005.

Steelers.com. "Official Site of the Pittsburgh Steelers," http://www.steelers.com/.

# ABOUT THE AUTHOR

**S**teve Hickoff is a lifelong Steelers fan who was born and raised north of Pittsburgh. A prolific writer, author, and editor, he also teaches college courses on media and American pop culture. Hickoff is a member of the Professional Football Researchers Association.